MY STORY – WRINKLES AND ALL

My Story – Wrinkles and All

Kathy Staff
with Liz Barr

Hodder & Stoughton

LONDON SYDNEY AUCKLAND

Copyright © 1997 by Kathy Staff

Foreword copyright © by Roy Clarke

First published in Great Britain 1997

The right of Kathy Staff to be identified as the Author of
the Work has been asserted by him in accordance with the
Copyright, Designs and Patents Act 1988.

10 9 8 7 6 5 4 3 2

All rights reserved. No part of this publication may be
reproduced, stored in a retrieval system, or transmitted,
in any form or by any means without the prior written
permission of the publisher, nor be otherwise circulated
in any form of binding or cover other than that in which
it is published and without a similar condition being
imposed on the subsequent purchaser.

British Library Cataloguing in Publication Data
A record for this book is available from the British Library

ISBN 0 340 69470 X

Printed and bound in Great Britain by
Mackays of Chatham PLC, Chatham, Kent

Hodder and Stoughton
A Division of Hodder Headline PLC
338 Euston Road
London NW1 3BH

Contents

Foreword

Some twenty-five or more years ago, I was enjoying the first flowering of a career I'd spent even more years preparing for. I was finally gaining acceptance as a writer – at first in radio and then television. My earliest work for television was for the drama departments of the then existing companies but because of a natural bias – even in drama – towards the comic I had recently been invited by the BBC to write a sitcom for them.

This was something I was more than keen to try and it resulted in a thirty-minute pilot script for a situation comedy which I called *Last of the Summer Wine*. It was written – or so I firmly believed – for three ageing men. Had I been asked at that time about any other characters in the piece likely to prove important to it in the event of its becoming a series, I wouldn't have given a thought to the part of the woman who was to play merely the neighbour of one of my three men. I felt sure this was just a bit part – which would continue to be just that – for an actress who would appear occasionally for a few seconds to be the foil of the actor who played the man-next-door. Her part figured not at all in my plans or hopes for the series.

How wrong I was.

In my own defence let me offer the excuse that my

priorities were those of a writer, and a fairly new writer at that. I believed overwhelmingly in the power of the words. I still do but I no longer underestimate the magic which the right performer brings to the right part.

I respected, of course, even then the importance of casting. I knew that the wrong choice of actor of any of my three men would seriously weaken and could destroy the whole piece. All my casting attention, therefore, went to these three and an excellent producer – James Gilbert – provided me with fortunate and happy results. As a consequence I hardly noticed who had been chosen, by him, to play the bit part of the female neighbour. This character was called Nora Batty and the actress selected to play her was Kathy Staff.

When I say I hardly noticed who had been chosen – that was only until she went to work and I found myself watching the first results and making mental notes to make more use of this actress's talents. Kathy's impact as Nora Batty was immediate. She hit exactly the right notes from word one and she has never faltered from them. But this was still very early days and although it was obvious to everyone that her part was already bursting out of its seams none of us realised how far it would grow.

The viewers knew. Kathy grabbed her audience from the first and they knew they loved her and they wanted more. It was an abiding lesson for me of the power of some performers to exceed their restraints; not in any overstraining way – by trying too hard, or reaching too far. Quite the opposite. But by being so absolutely right in a part that the sheer excellence of the combination of performer and part swells it beyond what might have been in lesser hands its bounds.

Even had I tried to continue with my original assumption that Nora Batty was a bit part, feedback from the viewers would soon have woken me up. They know a star when they see one. They can spot the magic of the right performer in the right part instantly – even if in the beginning she may be well down the cast list.

There is another role Kathy Staff plays rather well. (There are many others but this one's a bit special.) She is very good at being Kathy Staff, wife, mother, actress. People like her in this role too. She brings to it the same convincing strength of character. I've known Kathy for a good many years now and I've never seen a false note here either.

I can testify personally to the warmth and kindness of the woman. I remember with gratitude her kindness to my wife in sad circumstances.

Despite a lifetime in the arts there's little that's 'showbizzy' about Kathy. There's solid good sense and a calm not always to be found in our shaky professions. For me one of the attractions of this book will be its pointers to the factors which have enabled this woman to remain comfortably Kathy through all the invitations to the ego which success in her career has afforded.

Roy Clarke

1

Introducing . . .
Minnie Higginbottom

I was born at 243 Astley Street, in Dukinfield, Cheshire, on Potato Pie Day.

My mother had her household well regulated. Monday was Wash Day, Tuesday was Ironing, Wednesday was Cleaning the Bedrooms, Thursday was Baking and Potato Pie Day, and Friday was Cleaning Downstairs ready for the Weekend.

This was a Thursday, so my mother was baking bread and making her potato pie as usual. If you're from the North of England you'll know it, because we still have potato pie suppers here. It's really meat-and-onion-and-potato pie. You do it in a deep dish with a pastry crust on top.

We had a black grate, with the oven at the side. That's what most of the houses round here had in those days; you did your cooking in the oven at the side of the coal fire. You piled more coals on to get it really hot, or raked some away if you wanted a cooler oven – that was your temperature-control mechanism.

My mother had just finished baking her potato pie on this particular Thursday morning, when she started with labour pains. But the pie smelled so good, she thought, 'Oh dear. Well, I'm going to have my share before I send for the midwife, or else I shan't get any.'

So she sat down and ate a good plate of potato pie. *Then* she sent for the midwife, and I was born a few hours later. To this day, potato pie is one of my favourite dishes. I just love it.

My mother's name was Minnie and my father was Alfred Higginbottom. My mother's maiden name was Hartley. Her parents, Robert and Ada Hartley, had come from Manchester to settle in Dukinfield. Robert Hartley had a hardware business, with a warehouse in Manchester and a shop in Dukinfield, on Astley Street, on the corner of Robert Street, and they lived over the shop. My father's family had always lived in the Dukinfield area, and my father began his working life in the cotton-mills.

My parents met in church. That's how they met, because both families, the Hartleys and the Higginbottoms, attended St Mark's, Dukinfield, pronounced *Duck*-in-field. BBC announcers always say it as though it were 'Duke-in-field', but it's Dukinfield, and means 'field of the raven'. St Mark's church is nearly one hundred and fifty years old now, so it must have been quite a new church when my grandparents from both sides started going there.

I was born on 12 July 1928. My sister Constance was born on 9 May 1926, two years earlier. Connie was – and still is – very pretty and she had all the brains. I always say there was nothing left for me when I came along. Con had a little, turned-up nose and a pretty, round face, and her hair used to just wave without any problem. My hair has always been as straight as a die. It's quite thick and shiny and it looks all right with a fringe, but when I was little it was always scraped back under a grip. I always thought of myself as an ugly duckling, a plain Jane. I certainly never thought I was attractive. It wasn't all that important to me. Other things were far more important. Only I would have liked to have been – you know – a bit pretty.

Another irritating thing was that whereas Con grew tall, for a long time I was very small. I used to think I was going to be a dwarf, because nobody ever said, 'Coo, isn't Connie tall?' They always used to say, 'Aren't you small?' I used to think, 'Ooer. Perhaps I'm never going to grow.' But I'm quite average height now, five foot three and a half.

From the age of three I had only one ambition – to go on the stage – but what I wanted to be, originally, was a ballet dancer. That truly was my first ambition, and in a very funny way it was to be fulfilled much later, as I'll tell you in another chapter. One of my first public appearances was as an apple for the church fancy dress parade, and then, aged three, I was the fairy in the pantomime at our mission church. It was from that day on that I knew that all I wanted to do was to go on the stage. After being in that pantomime, going to school to learn about history, maths and geography was just a nuisance that had to be endured and got out of the way. The teachers weren't much help either, as far as I was concerned, because at first Con and I both went to the same school – St Mark's Junior and Infants – and they would keep saying to me, 'Your Connie would have known that,' or, 'Oh dear me, your Connie could have done that.' I got fed up with it. I thought, 'Oh well, let her do it then. Let her get on with it.'

I loved Con far too much to feel jealous of her. We've always been close, and never quarrelled, but at the same time I never wanted to follow in her footsteps.

I deliberately chose to be completely different, the opposite. Con was always reading, and loved doing her homework, whereas I couldn't wait to get out of doors and play. I had lots of friends in the neighbourhood. I was noisy and a tomboy. If there were trees to climb, I was there. I felt I could do anything the boys could do. We didn't have a garden at our first house on Astley Street – named after some Victorian bigwig called Lord Astley – but there was a big area at the back of the row of houses. It was not a field because there was no grass, and not really a yard, because there were no walls round; it was just a space, with toilets. We used to call it 'the back' and we played there. Sometimes, for real excitement, we used to go and swing round the lamp outside my grandparents' shop on the corner of Robert Street.

I was worse than my sister for getting into scrapes, and sometimes I couldn't be found when they wanted me to come in, but there was never any serious naughtiness. I kept pet ladybirds, until my father found my box full of them in a drawer. I'd got a cardboard box, made airholes in the lid, and given them leaves to eat. My father didn't think it was a good idea and I had to throw them away, which was very sad. I can't remember now whether it was because he thought it was cruel or unhygienic to keep them. I also liked 'Hairy Marys', our name for caterpillars that are covered in long hair. I collected them, too. A friend would look after them for me when we went away on holiday, and I would bring back a stick of Blackpool or Morecambe rock as payment. Unfortunately, I never managed to keep one long enough to watch it transform into a butterfly.

Con was more of a loner than I was, but she had her friends at school – all the quiet, studious ones like her. The 'goody-goodies', I thought them. At one time I thought she might be going to be a missionary as she was always so serious and good, but instead she became a teacher.

We were at 243 Astley Street, and Ada, my mother's younger sister, and my grandparents all lived with only three doors between, at 249 Astley Street, in the house behind their hardware shop. In 1930, when Ada married Arthur Bainbridge, a sign-writer with the London Midland and Scottish Railway Company, he had also come to live with them, so that Ada could go on helping her mother, who was deaf, in the shop. When my grandfather Robert died in 1933, Ada and Arthur stayed on.

I have one rather silly memory of those days. I was four, and my mother said to me, 'Come along and see what your Auntie Ada's got.' I remember going to their house and climbing the stairs – do you remember how steep stairs used to be when you were four? – thinking, 'I hope it's a big box of chocolates.' I went in and – it was a baby. My cousin Frances had been born. I was so disappointed. That's stuck with me all my life. I've never forgotten it, going in expecting to be given a chocolate, and it was just a baby. I suppose I must have got over it eventually, because Fran and I became very close and she's always been a good friend.

My cousins – Frances, Leonard and Margaret – were all born at 249 Astley Street, and then the family moved to Railway Street, where their youngest sister, Janet, was born. Even though they were all much younger than Con and me, it was more like having a younger brother and sisters than cousins. We all went to church together, to St Mark's. There were no backsliders, no black sheep in the family, and until very recently we had a big family choir of cousins, aunts, uncles, nephews and nieces still going strong at St Mark's.

When I was four and Con was six, the Rev. Edward Porter Tyson came to be our vicar. On the first Good Friday after he arrived, Mum and Dad were taking us to church as usual, and Mr Tyson met us as he was coming across from his vicarage. He said, 'You're not taking those small children into the three-hour service, are you?'

My parents said, 'Yes, we are.'

He said, 'Aah! Let them stay out and play with my two children at the vicarage.'

So we did. Billy Tyson was a few months older than Con, and I was a few months older than Muriel, so from then on they became very good friends of ours. Mr Tyson was a wonderful vicar, who stayed with us at St Mark's for eighteen years, until just before I got married. He was a very good friend to my family, and came back especially to marry us. His son Billy also became a vicar when he grew up, and I've been to open church fêtes for him. I really loved his father.

On Sundays, we children went to Sunday school at nine thirty in the morning. Church was ten thirty, then Sunday school again at two thirty, and then church again at six thirty. I was a normal child, so I did sometimes think it was too much. We weren't allowed to play with any toys; we were allowed only to either read a book or write a letter on a Sunday. We learned the catechism, which I don't think many children do now, and every Saturday we used to learn the collect, the special prayer for that Sunday. If you could say the collect word-perfect at Sunday school the next morning, you could win a special 'collect prize' at the end of the year, usually a Bible or a prayer book or some sort of special book. There were also 'good attendance' prizes, which you could choose. I won *Anne of Green Gables* once, I remember, for good attendance at Sunday school.

In 1933, when I was five, we moved a few doors along the road to 235 Astley Street, a larger house with a proper garden which was much nicer than just having 'the back'. The toilet was still outside, but only just. My parents did toy with the idea of putting a door through, but later on we had a bathroom and toilet made upstairs, so we had one loo outside and one upstairs. It was a lovely home, and my Dad loved his garden, so it was a very happy time.

My mother was always smart. I don't remember her ever looking unkempt. She always wore lovely shoes with Louis heels, with a handbag to match. Like me, she had inherited her family's strong jaw, but she was attractive. My father was handsome as a young man. I don't suppose he was very tall, about five foot nine, but slim, and they made a nice-looking couple. He had dark hair, and my mother was fair.

They were loving, affectionate parents. We were never afraid to go to them and talk to them. We had no secrets from them, except when we were saving up for a Christmas present for them. The lady at the corner shop, Mrs Howard, had a Christmas club, and Con and I used to put a halfpenny a week in, to buy my Dad a box of shortbreads, and my Mum a box of chocolates. We were always very secretive about this, although it can't have ever been too much of a surprise for them on Christmas morning, because we always got them the same things.

When I was christened, my mother had wanted to call me Leonora after her elder brother, my Uncle Leonard, who had been killed in the First World War. I wish she had, because I think it's such a nice name, but – and this is absolutely true, although I know you'll think I'm making it up – everybody said, 'Oh no! You can't call her that . . . everyone will call her "Nora".'

Nobody would agree to me being called Leonora, so my mother gave in, and called me by her own name, Minnie. So I began my life as little Minnie Higginbottom, and if she and I both felt a little disappointed, at least my mother was able to feel that she had done all that any mother could to spare her child the dreadful fate of having everyone calling her Nora.

2

Hard Times?

I suppose it was hard times when I was growing up in the thirties, but we children were never aware of that. It was a very happy time, although I wouldn't want to go back now to the days of outside loos. You had to go out into the 'back' to go to the loo, and it was so cold. You waited until you *had* to go. Some families didn't even have their own privy, and had to go quite a long way to a communal loo. People just accepted it. Everyone used to have potties under the bed for the night. Oh, yes! I've seen it all.

It's amazing how far things have moved. When we first started going abroad for holidays in the sixties it was the first time we had bathrooms 'en suite'. Whenever you stayed in a hotel in this country, it was just 'hot and cold in the bedroom' – if you were lucky – and a queue for the bathroom. But nowadays everywhere is en suite. People expect it, and quite right too. No, I wouldn't like to go back.

We were a reasonably prosperous working-class family. In many ways, I suppose we were quite well off. I don't think Mum and Dad had much money, but we always had enough. We were never a gambling family, but my mother had a few premium bonds, and she seemed to be quite lucky. But if ever she did get anything from them, she always shared it out with all the family. That's how we still are today; everyone shares their good fortune.

My mother made all our clothes. She was a lovely dressmaker. She'd buy the material to make herself a dress, and then make one each for Con and me. She even made our coats and hats, so she saved a lot of money that way.

When we grew out of our clothes, they were usually packed up and sent to the Salvation Army. When the war came and clothes were on coupons, our clothes were passed on to our younger female cousins. Even material was on coupons, and as children grow out of clothes so quickly, you couldn't afford not to pass them on within the family. Even our toys were handed down. I've had lots of letters over the years asking me if I have a favourite teddy bear I could auction for charity, but all our childhood toys went to our cousins, the Bainbridge children.

We never went short of anything. We had a nice home and good food. We had lots of friends, and we all went to the same school, because in those days you didn't pick and choose, you just went to the church school the nearest to you.

We always went on holiday every year. Not many other children round us went on holiday. They used to call us 'the nuts round the corner', because it was so unusual. People couldn't afford it. We originally went because my mother had had double pneumonia, with infection in both lungs, and she'd been told to get some sea air, so we went for a fortnight in Blackpool. Later we only went for a week because my father only had a week's annual holiday, so this first time was a gala holiday. We had to have 'the big cases' for two weeks. Father had to leave us to return to work after the first week; then he came back the following weekend to escort us home and help us with the cases.

We used to go by bus. We always stayed at a little boarding-house just along a little walkway beside the Imperial Hotel. We used to pass by the doors of the Imperial, and I used to think, 'One day, I'll go in there.' That was one of my ambitions. At our boarding-house, you just paid for the bedroom. My mother used to buy the food, and in the dining-room were sideboards. Each family had a little cupboard that was theirs, and they used to put the butter, bread and marmalade in there. If you wanted, Mrs Knight, the landlady, would cook your lunch or your evening meal, but you had to buy the meat and give it to her. We always went to Mrs Knight's, just at the back of the Imperial, two minutes from the north pier and the seaside.

There were donkey rides on the sands, and we always went on the pier every morning to hear Tony and the North Pier Orchestra. My mother loved them. It was threepence to get on the pier. Children were free, but my mother paid, and her threepence included a deckchair. She used to sit there quite happily for hours, listening to the music of Tony and the orchestra. We would wander off after a while and look at the penny slot machines.

Sometimes we went to Morecambe, but mainly Blackpool, and until the day she died, wherever my mother had been on holiday, she always had to have a few days at Blackpool or she hadn't 'been away'. You could have taken her to the south of France, but she would still want her few days at Blackpool.

For some people, times must have been very hard. The Manchester area was full of cotton-mills when I was a child, and my father originally worked there. There are none now; partly because in countries like India they can make cotton fabric so much more cheaply, partly because we had the strikes for higher pay in the twenties, which helped kill the industry. In those days, there was high unemployment and no welfare state.

Both my parents belonged to the Band of Hope when my father was a lay reader at Wharf Street Mission. They used to give lantern-slide lectures on the evils of drink, my father operating the slides while my mother read an improving story. Lots of people used to come. I suppose there was nothing much else to do. In those days people didn't have warm, comfortable homes to sit in. They didn't have electricity, so there was no heat or light, and they were glad to get out and meet in places that were warm and bright. I signed the pledge when I was a little girl, and I have never had an alcoholic drink in my life. When I started out as an actress lots of people said, 'Oh, we'll soon get you going.' But they never did, and I never have.

I can remember when the railways were nationalised. Nobody owned their own house in those days, we all used to rent, and our landlady, Mrs Booth, had shares in the railway. Her husband had died and left her his shares, which were her main source of income. When they nationalised the railway they gave her nearly nothing for them, they just took them. She was in a terrible state. She did own three houses, including ours, where the rent which she came to collect each week was eight shillings and sixpence. That was all she was left to live on, and even in those days that wasn't much.

The trains used to be great when I was a little girl, when they were all privately owned and all vying with each other: the London Midland and Scottish, the London North Eastern, and the Great Western Railways. They all used to try to give the best service. That's why I've always been a Conservative. People sometimes say to me in amazement, 'You? A Conservative?' But both sides of the family were in trade. My grandfather had his own business, and all my uncles and aunts had their shops and businesses. They all had to work hard and give good service to survive. So it's always seemed obvious to me that when people are competing they give better service.

In so many ways this century has been the most wonderful time in which to live. We used to go to Saturday morning cinema to see films called things like *Visit to Mars!* never dreaming we would one day sit at home watching real men landing on the real moon. Technology has just rocketed in my lifetime. Television has made us know what's going on all over the world. But I still say, 'The English, the English, the English are best. I wouldn't give tuppence for all the rest!'

I suppose the closest our family came to experiencing hard times was after the war, when my father came home very ill from the war. He wasn't expected to live for long, and couldn't work. He was entitled to a small army pension, but when he died my mother never thought of claiming it for herself. Then our next-door neighbour, Mr Matson, who was the manager of the local social security office, said to her one day, 'So the war was responsible for your husband's death?'

She said, 'Yes. He was perfectly fit before. He used to play football and even at one time thought of going professional.'

So he said, 'Come to see me at my office and we'll look into it.'

He managed to get her a war pension. It made a big difference to her. She was struggling rather until that happened, but she had never thought of claiming anything for herself. You didn't in those days.

3
Salt of the Earth – the Higginbottoms and Hartleys

I come from a real northern dynasty. If you were making up a fictional story about the North of England, my family had the names and the trades you'd invent for all your characters. As a matter of fact, my roots are probably quite similar to Nora Batty's, although hers would have been more rural.

My grandfather on my father's side was Alfred Higginbottom, and he was a boiler-maker. He used to have to go inside the big boilers to hammer them, and as a result he became stone deaf. When I knew him he didn't attend church because he couldn't hear what was going on, but my grandmother, Hannah Higginbottom, was a very staunch attender. Her sister Constance married my grandfather's brother, James Higginbottom, who was the other churchwarden at St Mark's with my maternal grandfather, Robert Hartley. You can see both their names on St Mark's church board if you're passing through Dukinfield and want to look in. So two sisters, Hannah and Constance Warrington, married two brothers, James and Alfred Higginbottom.

The Higginbottoms and the Hartleys were all born and brought up in and around the Dukinfield and Manchester area, all hard working stock, in trade, open all hours. It was the age of the tram. There were still horse-trams out of Manchester as far as Hyde and Ashton when I was born. You got the tram to either Hyde or Ashton and then walked to Dukinfield. I wonder how many people nowadays can remember the green-and-white trams with SHMD on the side – belonging to the Stalybridge, Hyde, Mossley and Dukinfield joint transport and electricity board – that went up almost as far as the moors before the war? Or, during the war, the khaki-coloured threepenny tickets in the shape of a Spitfire that you could buy from the conductor, which didn't take you anywhere on the old red-and-white Manchester trams, but all the money from them went towards the Lord Mayor of Manchester's Spitfire fund?

Now you're going to have to concentrate for this chapter, because it's like a Russian play with all the names. George Higginbottom, my father's eldest brother, was verger at St Mark's church, and he was also the caretaker at the church school, where first my father, and then Con and I all went, when it was a day-school for infants and juniors. Uncle George used to play Father Christmas at our Christmas party, and I could never understand why I was the only one in my class who was never allowed to go and see him. All the other children would sit on his knee to be given their presents, but they always said to me, 'No. Father Christmas has left you your present with your teacher.' I used to wonder so much about that. Why was I the only one who couldn't go and meet Father Christmas? No one ever told me until much later that it was because it was my uncle George, and I'd have recognised him.

The second Higginbottom son was my father, Alfred, who originally worked in a cotton-mill as an overlooker, but the damp badly affected his chest and he had to give it up. That's why the cotton-mills were all in Manchester originally, because of the damp atmosphere. After he had married my mother, my father began working for her father's hardware business, alongside two of her brothers, Robert and Peter, as commercial travellers.

Next in my father's family came Uncle Sam, who had a wonderful voice and sang in the choir. He was a baker. Sam and his wife Alice had a confectioner's shop. It was Alice's shop to begin with. When they married, Sam moved in and ran the business with her.

Then came my Auntie Alice, my father's younger sister, who'll be ninety on 31 December 1997. She married Tom Gregson, who was treasurer at one of the mills at Hyde. Tom worked in an office so he was 'a class above' really, but he died quite young, in his fifties, and Alice has been a widow for a long time now. They have two daughters, Ruth and Anne.

Then came Uncle Clem, who was a butcher. The Higginbottom family had a butcher and a baker both on King Street, Dukinfield, near the town hall. Clem married Doris, who was my favourite auntie.

My father had another younger sister, but she died as a child of pneumonia. So last but not least was the youngest Higginbottom, Uncle Harry, who is still going strong, and he married another Auntie Doris. He worked at the Co-op, in the grocery department.

Have you got all that? Now for my mother's family, the Hartleys. My maternal grandmother, Ada, was also stone deaf, like my father's father, but she was congenitally deaf. She had two earpieces with a band of wires going over her head, joining them. On her chest she had a big box with batteries in – it must have been at least five or six inches long and three inches wide – with a thing you spoke into. She could hear just a little if you shouted into that, and she could lip-read quite well. She used to serve behind the counter in their hardware shop on Astley Street, because my grandfather Robert Hartley, who was very inventive, rigged it up so that whenever people rang the bell, a light flashed.

My mother's immediate family are all gone now. They all served in the First World War, whereas my father and his brothers were all called up in the Second World War. My mother was four years older than my father, so she was a Red Cross nurse in the First World War, while he was too young to be called up. Just those few years made all the difference.

There was her eldest brother, Fred Hartley, who was very musical and played the organ for several different churches. There used to be a Fred Hartley who broadcast music on the radio and they used to tease him, but it wasn't him. The next brother was Leonard, who my mother had wanted to name me after. Leonard had been going into the ministry after the 1914–18 war, and they were all very proud of him because he would have been the first member of the family to be ordained, but it wasn't to be.

In order of ages it was Fred, Leonard, Robert, my mother Minnie, Peter and lastly Auntie Ada, the baby, eleven years younger than my mother. The two younger sons, Robert and Peter, and later my father as well, used to work for my grandfather's hardware business, travelling round getting in orders for the first three days of each week, and in the evenings they would take their order-books back to the Manchester warehouse, where my mother and Ada would make them up ready for the three men to deliver on Thursday and Friday. Then they started all over again the following Monday.

After my grandfather died, Uncle Robert went to live in Denton, and Uncle Peter went to live in Salford, so we didn't see so much of them after that, except when they came over for family reunions. It doesn't sound very far now, but travel was much more difficult in those days. None of us had cars, so you easily lost touch. Peter changed to travelling in toys, so he was always very popular with the younger generation of the family whenever he came over for a visit.

When we were very tiny, before they all began to move away, I remember how we all used to gather at my Grandma's house on Astley Street every Sunday after church. Both sides of the family were devout Anglicans, and everybody has remained Anglican as far as I know, although my cousin Letty, Robert's daughter, did go to chapel for a while.

My mother had an extremely beautiful singing voice, a remarkable voice, and if she had been trained she could have sung professionally, in opera. She won a scholarship to Hyde Grammar School but she didn't go, because her sister Ada, being eleven years younger, still needed looking after, and my grandmother needed my mother to help in the shop and at home.

My mother sang in a quartet, and she used to do a lot of charity shows, but she never sang professionally. When we went on holiday and the Salvation Army band would come and play hymns on the sands, my mother would always go and join in. She had such a loud and beautiful voice, Con and I used to hide so that nobody would know that we were connected with her. I only wish I'd thought to make a recording of her singing, because she really did have such a beautiful voice.

My grandfather, Robert Hartley, was a man ahead of his time. He ran a boys' club, under one of the railway arches on Cooper Street before the First World War, one of the first of its kind. He even went to America, an unheard of thing in those days, and he was one of the first people to have a cat's-whisker radio. He made everybody listen, 'Shhhh! Shhh!'

He also started his own mission, in the Tame Valley, which for some reason everyone always called 'the Cuckoo Square Mission'. It was in one of the worst areas in town, and he rented this little cottage, because like I've said, nobody thought of owning property in those days. It was such a rough area, the Tame Valley, that the police had to go down in twos. My mother and Auntie Ada used to go round selling parish magazines, and they said they always felt quite safe, but the police didn't dare go down alone.

St Mark's church, Dukinfield, also grew out of a mission church, the Wharf Street Mission. When the numbers grew larger, the mission applied to the Chester diocese for permission to build a church. The only Anglican church in the area was right on the border with Stalybridge; it actually is *in* Stalybridge, although it is called St John's, Dukinfield. The bishop gave the go-ahead, and so the people from the Wharf Street Mission actually built St Mark's church themselves, nearly one hundred and fifty years ago, the church to which my family and I have belonged all my life.

My grandfather and later my father were both lay readers at the Wharf Street Mission, which continued to function in parallel with St Mark's for some years after the new church was built. The congregation at the mission would go and join the people at St Mark's once a month for a service of Holy Communion. We always went to the mission, and it was where I was a fairy in their pantomime, aged three. But eventually it was closed down and everyone went to St Mark's.

Another unusual thing that Robert Hartley did was to give each of his six children an American organ as a wedding present. They were beautiful, built of mahogany, with little mirrors. I don't know where on earth he could have got them from, but every one of his children got one, so we had one. The keyboard was just the same as a piano, with foot pedals and blowers.

Most of his children could play. Uncle Fred was a very good musician, and Uncle Leonard used to play. All that generation of the family are dead now, and I think the organs just faded away. They'd be worth a fortune today if any of them had been kept, but none of them were.

We had ours until I left home to go on the stage, and when I came back a few months later it had gone. I said, 'Where's the organ gone?'

Mum said, 'Oh, well, it was getting to look a bit shabby.'

My father had dismantled it and used the wood in his greenhouse. I felt very sad, because it was something that had always been there.

So there they all were then, in the years before the war, the Hartleys and the Higginbottoms, all in trade, all staunch Christians, all northerners. The salt of the earth you'd have thought them, and the backbone of Britain. Hitler didn't really think he had a chance against that little lot, did he?

4

The Day the Lights Came on

In 1995, I got a letter from a national newspaper. As part of the celebrations for the fiftieth anniversary of VE day, newspapers and radio stations were all writing to celebrities who had been alive then, asking if they could remember what they were doing and where they were on the day the war ended. I could hardly think of a thing. I did remember very vaguely that we had had a bonfire in my Grandma's 'back', and that there was dancing on the front of Dukinfield Town Hall, where there's a big platform. But it wasn't very vivid in my mind at all.

The thing that *was* vivid was how – suddenly – all the lights came on. All my formative years had been spent in darkness. The bombing didn't start straight away, but we had black-out from day one. You weren't allowed to show any light at all. You daren't have a crack of light showing through your window or you could be fined. The streets were all dark. Traffic lights just had a little slit in the middle to show whether it was the green, amber or red. None of the street lights were ever on. The shop lights were never on. We used to have a little torch, if we were out at night, just a tiny, faint beam to show us where we were walking.

Then, suddenly, there was all this light. There was

a song we used to sing, 'When the lights go on again all over the world' but of course the lights hadn't gone on. When they did, it was the most marvellous, unforgettable thing, to see the whole place lit up.

I was eleven when the war started, and Uncle Clem, the butcher, was marrying his Doris the following day. They had planned to hold the reception in the school, which was always used as a church hall, but they didn't have any black-out curtains there, and the only place that did was the working men's club. So Con and I spent the whole morning carrying all the food across from the school to the club.

Soon after that Clem was called up, and poor Auntie Doris had to keep the butcher's shop going, when she didn't know a thing about how to do it. She was only twenty-two and she was my favourite auntie. We often used to go to the cinema together. I went along to see her one Wednesday, when we were supposed to be going out, but she said she couldn't go, because she had to find out how to make sausages. I said, '*Sausages?*'

She said, 'People keep coming in the shop and asking me for sausages, but I don't know how to make them. I've seen Clem do them, but I can't remember how he did it.'

So we spent the whole evening with all this sausage meat. There was a sausage-making machine, and we could get the meat into the skins. We got that far, but then they kept splitting open when we were trying to tie the knots. And she kept saying, 'No, no. That's not right. Not right at all.'

It was very messy and very frustrating. At about ten o'clock I had to go home. Doris eventually went to bed, and tossed and turned. Then, at three o'clock in the morning, it suddenly struck her – the secret was in the twisting. She'd had a mental flash of seeing Clem giving them each a little twist. She went straight down to the shop and started twisting – in the middle of the night – and she managed it. They were a bit uneven at first, some were long and some were short, and some were much fatter than others, but at least she'd got her sausages made. So that was one hurdle my Auntie Doris got over during the war.

Another auntie, Nellie, and her son Norman were caught in an air-raid at York. Well, Nellie wasn't a real auntie, but she would have been, because she had been engaged to my Uncle Leonard. After he was killed, she married Jack Harrop, who worked at Dukinfield wagon-works. During the war the works were transferred to York to help make and repair railway carriages, so they'd had to move to York, but then her husband died. On the day of the York bombing, Auntie Nellie and Norman heard the air-raid siren and rushed along with everyone else into the shelters, but when the all-clear sounded they discovered that neither of them had got the key to their house, and they had no idea where they had left it. They searched all the way down the path, went back inside the shelter, looking everywhere they'd been. They couldn't find it at all. Finally they decided they would just have to go back home and see if they could get in through a window. They got back to the house – and every single window and door had been blown in. They stood there looking at it, and just shrieked with laughter. In those days you had to laugh at these things, or else you'd never stop crying.

On the Sunday before Christmas in 1940, we were

having a party at my Grandma's. We always had a family gathering at Grandma Higginbottom's at Christmas, and she used to put little silver threepenny bits in the mince pies. Uncle George always had a half-a-crown in his, which was something else I never understood – how he always seemed to contrive to get the mince pie with the half-a-crown. My grandfather, who was absolutely stone deaf, went out into 'the back' to go to the toilet. A moment later we saw him standing outside, waving and shouting, 'Come on, Mother! There's a wonderful display over at Bellevue.'

It was Manchester going up in flames, the Manchester blitz. We couldn't get him back in. We were all shouting *'Come in!'* but it was dark, and he couldn't hear us. 'Look! It's beautiful!' he kept saying, watching the bombs.

Poor Granddad. He never quite understood what was going on. Of course he knew there was a war; he read the papers, and all his sons were in the services, but he was old. He was so used, every year, to there being the most wonderful firework display at Bellevue, and I suppose he went out in the yard, and saw these bright lights in the sky and thought that that was what it was. Manchester was devastated by bombs for two days before Christmas in 1940, and again on 9 January 1941. We were left alone after that, until the IRA decided to come and have another go last year. The people who have suffered most this time are all the small shopkeepers, and I feel very upset for them.

Uncle Harry and Uncle Sam were sent overseas a few days after the D-Day landings, and my father was called up a few months after that. He was forty years old, and one of the very last batch to be called. He had recently been made assistant manager of a Bradford company called Provident Clothing and Supply Company, running their Ashton office, and he thought he would be too old for the army. It was a pity really that they took the forty-year-olds, but I suppose they needed everybody.

Unfortunately, instead of giving him an office job, where he would have been very useful with his age and management experience, he was put in the Royal Artillery and, because he could drive, they made him a batman driver. He ended up driving all the way through France into Germany, part of the front that was pushing the Germans back. Sometimes he had to sleep outside, under the vehicle, at his age, and with his weak chest from working in the mills. He was in Germany, and had just gone into a river for a swim on a hot day when he was suddenly taken seriously ill. He always said that it was a German boy who saved his life, by getting him out of the water in time. He had a cerebral thrombosis. The army flew him straight back to England and discharged him, so they got him off their hands that way. They gave him a small pension. The doctor told my mother that he wouldn't ever be able to work again, and he could go at any time.

I know many people think we shouldn't have wars, and if you are a Christian you shouldn't fight, but there comes a time when so many wicked things have been done that somebody has to put a stop to it. We had God on our side, I'm sure of that. If Hitler had invaded Britain in the early years he would have won, because we weren't nearly ready for him. He just walked through all the other countries. *Dad's Army* is all very well for a laugh on the television, but I don't think we could possibly have stopped the Germans if they'd invaded, but God sent them the other way, to Russia. Don't tell me that was nothing to do with the Almighty, because I don't believe it.

From our church we only lost four. On each Remembrance Sunday the vicar reads out the names. There must have been forty or fifty St Mark's boys killed in the First World War, but only four in the second. But this time we had all been in the front line, all been bombed. And, like so many others, although he wasn't killed outright in action, the war was ultimately responsible for my father's death.

When they got him home they said he shouldn't work or do anything that would affect his brain, but when he recovered sufficiently he said, 'I can't just sit around'.

We had a big ropeworks in Dukinfield, Kenyon's Ropeworks, and our vicar at St Mark's, Mr Tyson, persuaded them to give him a job there. He used to sit and untwine the rope. It wasn't what he'd been used to.

He had attacks, with terrible pain. It didn't affect him all the time. He had a slight limp, that was all. Most of the time you wouldn't have known how bad he was. It didn't affect his speech or anything, so he was perfectly normal except when he was having an attack. My mother had been a nurse during the First World War, and her motto was, 'Not sympathy – treatment', so as soon as he had one of his attacks she used to start the treatment long before the doctor arrived.

He managed to keep going, with her help, for sixteen years after the war, which nobody had thought he would do, and I'm sure if it weren't for my mother, he wouldn't have done. He even managed to better himself a little, but he never got back to the sort of management jobs he'd been used to. We were all living in Dukinfield when he died. I was married and had my two little girls, Katherine and Susan, by then. I used to meet Katherine from the church school and walk down to my mother's, because we all lived near the church. It was January. We were sitting round the fire together, the children were playing on the floor, I was next to my Dad, and we'd just had a cup of tea. He put his cup down and as he sat back his head fell back. My mother said, 'What's the matter, Alfred? Are you all right?'

He didn't gasp, he didn't do anything, and he was dead. I was sitting next to him and I had no idea. I turned to look at him, and he'd gone. I think I knew, but you hope you're not right. I put the children in the kitchen and I said, 'Now, you two, stay in there, because Granddad's ill.' Uncle Clem's wife, Auntie Doris, had a sister Mary with a little grocery shop in Astley Street, so I ran in there and said, 'Would you ring for the doctor? My Dad's had an attack', and I ran back.

My Uncle Clem arrived soon afterwards, and as soon as he saw him he just said, 'Oh my God, he's gone,' and picked him up like a baby and put him on the bed. When the doctor arrived, he confirmed that he was dead. He was sixty in the November, and he died in the January. He was, like so many of his comrades even to this day, a late casualty of the war.

I think, when I was young, life was very small. We didn't have television, we barely listened to the radio.

We only knew what was happening in our little particular area. Life was going to school, coming home, going to church on Sunday and meeting the family. The entire world was Dukinfield. Nothing else really existed, apart from once a year going to Blackpool or Morecambe.

The war changed everything. I was seventeen when it finished, so all my developing years were during the war. I think my generation were all affected by it. I used to go to the cinema and watch the *Pathé News*, and for the first time I began to see things happening in other parts of the world, and realised that the rest of the world was real.

In the war years, there weren't the 'teenage' fashions that they have nowadays. You were just an 'in between'. We either looked old-fashioned in grown-up women's dresses, or like big Shirley Temples in children's clothes and short socks. I wanted to be like the film star, Ann Sheridan. I thought she was beautiful, but not in a pretty-pretty way. She had character in her face. I used to put my hair in sweeps like hers when I could – it was the wartime fashion – but I'm afraid there was no real resemblance. I used to think, 'Oh, I wish I could look like her.' But there we are. I never could, and never did.

I didn't feel like an adult at seventeen, when the war ended. Some things, however, I had made my mind up about. I knew that I was going to be an actress, and I knew that when I was old enough I would vote Conservative. I didn't have a vote, but I was already a staunch Conservative.

I thought I'd go and live abroad when Churchill lost the election in 1945, I was so appalled. I thought

I couldn't live in this country if it voted out Churchill after all he'd done. I won't say he alone won the war for us, but having such a strong leader made all the difference. He made us all believe that we'd win. Even when Hitler had overrun the whole of Europe and we were on our own, before the Americans came in, none of us doubted for one minute that we'd win in the end.

There was a general feeling after the war – from the homecoming soldiers, the munitions workers and lots of people – the feeling that 'it's our time now', time for the man in the street to have some say in running the country. But because there had been an earlier coalition with Churchill in it, I think a lot of people just assumed that whichever party won the election, Churchill would still be the Prime Minister, so they didn't realise they were voting him out.

I started work as a professional actress four years later. I was playing the part of the old mother in *The Chiltern Hundreds*, where somebody mentions 'the Prime Minister', and I had to put in, 'Mr Churchill . . .,' and they said, 'Mother! Churchill's not the Prime Minister.'

My character said, 'As long as Mr Churchill is alive, he will *always* be the Prime Minister.'

That was exactly how I felt, too.

5

Making My Name

Here's to our Minnie
  Star overnight
As dear young Miranda –
  No trace of stage fright
She worships Bing Crosby
  Ron Reagan and Flyn –
Who knows, one of these days
  We may worship . . . Min!

I have never had any actual training for the theatre,
except for just doing it. I was what you'd call 'a natural'.
I always enjoyed reading, but as I've said, I was never
in the least bit interested in putting much effort into
things like maths. After junior school, Con went on to
Hyde Grammar, while I went to Lakes Road Secondary
Modern – where from the start I was very keen and
industrious only when it came to learning my parts in
the school plays. I was in all of them.

My mother sent me for private singing lessons while
I was still at school, and my teacher, Harold Burgess,
insisted that I also learn to play the piano. He was
the organist at Ashton Parish Church, and he took
private pupils in his studio in the centre of Ashton.
I think my mother sent me partly because she knew

that everything to do with performing was where my heart lay, and partly because it was the one thing that she had always wished she'd done herself – been trained as a singer. I don't have nearly as good a voice as my mother had – she was really outstanding – but at least singing was one thing I could do a bit better than my sister.

Con went straight to Sheffield University when she left Hyde Grammar. I eventually became head girl at Lakes Road, because even though I was completely uninterested in my schoolwork, I've always been quite an organised person. The headmistress, Mrs Wood – who got the MBE for the work all of us at our school did, sending parcels to the troops – said to my mother, 'Minnie could organise a whole office. I don't suppose anybody would allow her to do it, but she could – she's got the capabilities.'

I suppose that's what made my mother think I should do a secretarial course when I left school at fourteen, naturally without having sat a single examination. Mother insisted that I had to have something behind me, some sort of training, before I started trying to look for work in the theatre, so I took a shorthand and typing course at Stamford Commercial College in Ashton, at the top of Stamford Street, and although I was never very fast at taking down shorthand, I could usually manage to read it back, and I think my early piano lessons must have helped me to become really quite good at typing.

Meanwhile I had joined the Oldham Repertory Theatre Club, although not to act. You had to be a member of the repertory theatre club before you could even buy tickets to go to see the plays, it was so good and so popular. You often had to wait twelve months before there was a vacancy. I put my name down as soon as I left school, and at sixteen I was accepted as a member.

From then on my cousin Fran and I used to go every week to Oldham Rep. It was wonderful. I've still got all my old programmes. There were the regular 'stars' who we saw every week. Joan Heath was the greatest, to my mind. She was the leading lady, and I have never, ever, seen her give a bad performance. She really inspired me when I was sixteen, sitting in the audience. She used to play all sorts of parts. One week she would play the elegant lady, and the next week she might be the comedy grandma. That was the kind of actress I aspired to be.

We also used to get visiting 'big names'. Marius Goring came, I remember, with his wife, Lucy Manheim, to do three plays. It all had a big influence on me. I used to think that if I could ever play at Oldham Rep, I would have reached the height of my ambition. I'd know that I was really there, that I'd made it.

At sixteen, after completing my secretarial course, my first job was working for ten shillings a week at the National. Not the National Theatre, unfortunately. This was the National Gas and Oil Engine Company Limited, in Ashton-under-Lyne. Luckily, soon after I joined them, the firm started an operatic and dramatic society. They said they were going to audition everybody who wanted to come along and read. The first play they were doing was *Quiet Wedding*. I went along to the auditions, very excited . . . and I was the only person who wasn't asked to read. I had gone along with two friends, both very pretty girls with curly hair, and we were all going to read for the part of Miranda, the young bridesmaid. My friends both went in before me, and they gave one the part of Miranda and the other was made her understudy, and I wasn't even given the chance to read. They just came out and announced the casting. I was heartbroken. Ever since then, whenever I have had anything to do with casting a production, I've always insisted that *everybody*, whether they look right or not, reads, because you don't know.

However, they said, 'Now we've cast it and we've also cast all the understudies, so if you've been given a part but can't attend a rehearsal, you must arrange for your understudy to be there.'

They were very professional about it, and made everyone rehearse nearly every night after work. They'd been rehearsing for about a week when the two girls came to me together and said, 'We both want to go to a dance tomorrow night, but there's another rehearsal for the play. Would you go and read our part?'

So of course I said, 'Yes,' and I went along and read their part at the rehearsal the next night. The next day at work it was up on the notice-board: *There is to be an emergency meeting of the casting committee tonight. Any changes will be announced tomorrow.*

The following morning it went up on the notice-board that I'd got the part of Miranda. I don't think either of the other two girls really minded. They were far more interested in going to parties and having fun. And after the play was over, at the celebration party, everyone signed the card I've quoted at the beginning of this chapter, so there can't have been any hard feelings.

It was an operatic and dramatic society, so the next year we put on a musical, *The Arcadians*, and all the people who had had parts in the play the year before could only be in the chorus, so that other people could have a leading part.

The following year we did another play, *This Happy Breed*, and they cast me, who by now had reached the grand old age of eighteen, as the grandmother, old Granny Flint. I absolutely adored playing Granny Flint. They had a proper make-up artist, Gordon Scott, who was very good. He didn't do lines, he did shading, to make me look old.

After that I was inundated with requests from other amateur dramatic societies. In those days, many of the amateur societies were as good as professional companies. Sometimes I would be rehearsing for five different shows at a time, nearly always playing character parts. I became the world's greatest living expert at making myself up to look old. After a time I joined Ashton Rep where we did a play a month. We used to rehearse for three weeks and then perform each play for a full week.

My mother said I was treating her house as an hotel. I used to arrive home late, go to bed, then off to work in the morning, then straight to a rehearsal. She always came to see me. I think she thought I was good, but she never said a lot. She never said, 'You were marvellous,' or anything like that. I think my family just expected me to be good. I'd been in all the plays at school, and this was the thing they knew I was good at.

A year later, aged nineteen, I joined Joshua Heap and Company. It was a smaller engineering firm than the National, but I was secretary to the managing director, so it was better money. It was very old-fashioned, and as Dickensian as the name sounds. The accounts books were huge, and they used to heave them down from the shelves to put them on the desk, where they wrote in all the figures in ink. I was there for nearly two years, until I was twenty-one.

All this time I had been writing off to different theatre companies who advertised in the *Stage*. I used to send the picture I'd had taken of myself as Granny Flint, because I was always interested in playing 'character' parts. I didn't want to be an actress for the glamour, or out of a desire to be the leading lady. I just loved acting, becoming different characters. I wanted to do it for my living.

But if I wanted to make my name, the first thing I would have to do was to *change* my name. Nobody in the theatre would have looked at you with a name like Minnie – Minnie Higginbottom especially. They'd have thought, 'Oh my goodness, whoever's this?' It was long before the days when Albert Finney and Maggie Smith became famous.

I wanted to be a Katherine, not for any special reason, but because it was just a name I've always loved. Con and I were travelling together on the bus to Oldham Rep one day, and we were talking about this and she said, 'If you're having Katherine, you need a small name to go with it. What about Brant, look?' because we were just passing a shop called Brant's. So that was the name I took, Katherine, the name I loved, and Brant, the name of the shop we passed on the bus.

In the *Stage*, I saw an advertisement that looked promising, from a company called the Kinloch Players for a 'student-actress'. They were a Scottish touring company who operated up in Aberdeenshire. They accepted me. Stupid me, not having attended to my geography lessons, I didn't realise how far from home I would be travelling. I had thought, 'Scotland. That's up north. Good. That's near me.' Auntie Doris and Uncle Clem made sure I got off all right. They took me in their car to the station in Manchester and put me on the train for Aberdeen.

I'd never left home before, never been anywhere without my parents or Con for company. Never mind, they had agreed to take me on, and in 1949 at the age of twenty-one, Katherine Brant had got her first professional engagement. I had my foot on the bottom rung of the ladder.

My mother and father's wedding, 1924.
From left to right: Alice, my father's sister; my father, Alfred; my mother, Minnie;
Sam, my father's brother; Ada, my mother's younger sister.

Me, aged about one, 1929.

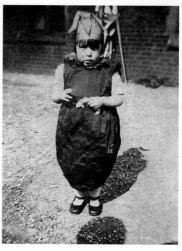

My first public appearance, in 1931,
as an apple!

With my sister Connie (right), 1931.

A pantomine at Wharf Street Mission, 1934. I was a fairy and am in the front row, fifth from the left. Connie, who was a soldier, is immediately behind me.

With my mother (centre) and
Connie (right), 1941.

From left to right: me, John,
my father, my mother and Connie at
Sheerness, 1950.

John and me on our wedding day, 18 August 1951,
with John's parents (on the left) and my parents (on the right).

Strolling down the promenade at Sheerness with John, 1950.

John and me with Sheila and Jim Burton at Scarborough, 1954.
(You can tell it's Scarborough by the windbreak!)

My first real part (at the National Theatre!) as Miranda the bridesmaid in *Quiet Wedding*, 1944.

Susan (aged 2½) and Katherine (aged 4½), 1961.

As Granny Flint (aged 80) in *This Happy Breed* at Ryecroft School,
Ashton-under-Lyne, 1946.

With Roy Barraclough as Harry and Lorna Everett in *Castle Haven*, 1969–70.

As Mrs Watty in *The Corn is Green* with
John Jardine and Sheila Price at Oldham Rep, 1970.

As Vera Hopkins in *Coronation Street*, 1974.

As Doris Luke in *Crossroads*, 1978.

With Eamonn Andrews on *This is Your Life*, 1984.

6

The Bottom Rung

In Scotland I was homesick at first. Another student-actor, George Bancroft, who was taken on at the same time, came from near Blackpool, and his parents sent him the local newspapers with all the coverage of switching on the Blackpool Illuminations. He showed me the pictures and, as we sat together looking at them, we both very nearly cried. But it didn't last long. We were kept far too busy to think about missing life at home.

We were the Kinloch Players. Henry Parker and his wife, Mary Kinloch, were the actor-managers of the troupe, which toured the villages of Aberdeenshire. When I first arrived the company was at Kemnay, and then we moved on to Rhynie by Huntly, and we stayed there for the rest of my time with them.

We had theatrical skips, big baskets, and when we moved from one village to the next we put all the costumes in the skips and piled them up on the lorry. We didn't carry much in the way of scenery, but we had curtains and lights, and we had to pack everything up on the lorry and then sit high up on top of it all ourselves to travel to the next village. It was wonderful, riding through the Scottish countryside in the sunshine on top of the lorry, singing. Suddenly George hurled himself at me, shoving my head down. He just saved me from being decapitated by telegraph wires.

I was earning two pounds a week. I had to pay my board out of that, thirty bob, so that left me ten shillings a week. The only training we got, as 'students', was having to do everything. We did a different play every night. There were two hundred people in Rhynie by Huntly, so it meant we were getting quite good numbers into the plays; often a hundred came to see each play. There was nothing else to do in the village. There was no electricity in most of the homes, although there was in the hall where we were. Even there we had Tilley paraffin lamps that they used to pump up. But with only such a limited potential audience, everyone who wanted to see a play would come for the 'first night', so if we wanted them back we had to do a different play the next night.

Henry Parker and Mary Kinloch knew all the plays backwards, but the rest of us had a lot to learn. It was unbelievably hard work. We used to get the scripts last thing at night after the performance, to learn before the following day. Then we'd spend the next day rehearsing, and put it on that night. Then we'd be given the next one to learn. If a play was running short, Henry Parker would sometimes say to me, 'You'd better change into evening dress and come on and sing a couple of numbers.' Or he'd say, 'We'll put a bit of comedy in, we'll do the routine with you coming in with a shopping bag . . .' and we'd put a little comedy sketch in the middle of the play.

I did once have a whole weekend to prepare for a play, because it was to run for two nights. We were doing *Snow White and the Seven Dwarfs* and Mary Kinloch was Snow White. She must have been well into her forties. I was the Wicked Queen. I also had to train seven local children to be the dwarfs. It was hard! These children had never seen anyone dancing, let alone tried to do it themselves. At home in Dukinfield, doing a pantomime every year, virtually all the children from church knew at least a few little steps, but these children hadn't a clue even how to move one foot after the other in time to music. I had to get all their costumes ready, washed and ironed, make sure they fitted and alter them where necessary, to say nothing of learning the part of the Wicked Queen.

We performed *Snow White* for two nights, Monday and Tuesday, and of course the entire village population were in for that, to see the children. They were nearly fighting for seats.

George Bancroft was playing the Woodcutter who the Wicked Queen sends to get Snow White's heart to prove that she's dead. I was doing my soliloquy to the mirror,

> Mirror, mirror on the wall,
> Who is the fairest of them all?

I can't remember exactly, but he should have come on and said something like,

> In this casket lies her heart.

Then my next line completed the rhyme, with something like,

Now who can stop my evil art?

Poor George came flying on – he only had one line in the whole thing and I'd done pages and pages to the mirror and all of that – but he went to pieces and said, 'Um. Er . . . Her heart's in this box!'

I thought, 'Now what do I do?'

I saved the day by repeating the line he should have said:

What? In that casket lies her heart?
Now who can stop my evil art?

It was wonderful training if you could stand the pace, but it was a hard life, and lots of hopeful young actors with stars in their eyes became very discouraged by the amount of work you had to do, and would fall by the wayside. I loved every moment of it.

They're a funny lot in Scotland. They used to say to me, 'When you go back to England, you tell the government . . .' as though as soon as you were in England you were in London and could go and 'tell the government' what they should be doing. I could see myself stalking up to the Queen or the Prime Minister and saying, 'Excuse me. I thought you ought to know, the people in Scotland are not happy.' I'd actually only been to London once in my life, for a holiday before the war.

James Hartley (no relation) came up to see one of our productions. He was the northern critic for the *Stage*, and afterwards he came to see me backstage and said how much he'd enjoyed my performance. He had set out for Dundee to see Richard Todd, who was an up-and-coming star then, and he had only quite by chance decided to come further north to look in on us. Later he called in again, to see another of our productions. Afterwards he said to me, 'You shouldn't stay here too long.' I suppose he thought that with doing a different play every night, if I stayed too long I'd go barmy.

He gave me a whole pile of his business cards – James Hartley, Northern Critic for the *Stage* – and on the back of each of them he'd written, 'Katherine Brant is a very good, very versatile artist.' He said that when I was writing away to apply for other jobs, I should include his cards. I've still got a couple of them.

Before I got started in Scotland I'd applied for hundreds of different acting jobs, with no success. It was the old catch-22 – until you had had some experience no one wanted to take you on, but you couldn't get any experience until they did. But now, not only did I have some experience, with the Kinloch Players, I also had James Hartley's cards. It all worked out, and in the autumn of 1949 I joined a company with the very grand name of the International Players, who were then doing a season in Llanelli.

It was an important moment in my life, moving to Llanelli. I've called it the bottom rung of the ladder, my time in Scotland, but I don't think that I was really even on the bottom rung, it was so low. Everything changed for the better when I joined the International Players at Llanelli, South Wales. This was the big-time at last, for I was now in a theatre company doing a season of *weekly* rep, the same play for a whole week; and it was also where I was to fall in love.

7

The 'International' Set

It was quite a journey from Aberdeenshire down to South Wales. I wanted to go home first, to have a day or two to gather my strength, and to see how my father was getting on, because he was still very poorly. Henry Parker was annoyed. He said he thought that if I was leaving the Kinloch Players, I should go straight to Llanelli. He even said to me, 'Your type shouldn't be in our business, if you want to go home more than to get on with your work.' Anyhow, I did go home, but I didn't stay long.

It's a hard life, doing repertory acting, so you have to love it, and I did love it – every minute of it. I didn't care how hard I worked. Having come from a very comfortable home, some of the digs left a lot to be desired, but it didn't bother me. I was healthy and strong, which you had to be. I was earning four pounds a week with the International Players, twice what I'd been getting as a student-actress, and doing weekly rep, with a whole week to learn the lines, after so many months of doing a different play every night, so it seemed like heaven to me.

Every Monday night, after the 'first night', you were given the next week's play. You'd start rehearsals for that on the Tuesday morning. You'd have it blocked –

that means you'd learn when and where to come on, all your moves on stage, all the places you had to stand, where the furniture would be, where and when you had to exit. You'd carry on rehearsing on Wednesday, Thursday and Friday, with a technical rehearsal on Saturday, dress-rehearsal Monday afternoon, and play it Monday night. Then you'd start again on Tuesday, blocking in your next part for the next production. At night you were on stage acting one character, and by day you were rehearsing as another character. There was hardly any time to remember who you were yourself.

We didn't have any stars, we all just played 'as cast' whatever part we were given. I was very happy doing that. One week I'd play the batty old grandmother, and the next week I might be a glamorous young thing. You didn't have time for jealousy or to worry about whether you should be in a different part, or petty things like that. You had to get on with what you had to do. It was fantastic training. I've always enjoyed the character work, so I never hankered after the leads, but by the end of my time with them I was playing a lot of leads. They were even saying, 'We're doing such and such a play, what part would you like?' and allowing me to choose. So I suppose I must have been doing all right.

I did feel I was getting my foot more firmly on the ladder. My first major role was when we started doing *Hobson's Choice*, and I played Maggie, one of my favourite parts because she's someone with whom I can easily identify. The play is set in Salford, so the characters were almost real to me, coming from so close to home, and it's all about running a shop, a way of life

I knew very well from all my uncles and aunts. As a touring repertory company, we put on *Hobson's Choice* wherever we went, and I always played Maggie. It's a marvellous part and I'm only sorry that I'm too old to play it now.

One of the funniest moments was at the first night of *The Barretts of Wimpole Street*. I was playing Elizabeth Barrett, who has a dog, Flush. Flush was played by Sally Bradley. John Bradley was the leading man, and Sally was his own dog, a little Pekinese. She had to sit at the bottom of the bed, and was always terrified until John came on, as Robert Browning. As soon as she heard John's voice she was perfectly happy.

We were doing the scene where we've come back together from my first walk, and he puts me down on a chaise longue. We then had a love scene, and he had to get down on one knee and propose. I took my hat off and put it down beside me, whereupon Sally, who until then had been sitting quite pleased and well behaved at the bottom of the chaise longue, suddenly picked my hat up and started throwing it in the air, all through our romantic love scene. The audience was shrieking, and John, who was kneeling with his back to the audience, was shaking with laughter. I stalked over to the fireplace, where we had a bell-pull, and I pulled it, for the maid. The girl playing Wilson the maid was standing in the wings and she hissed at me, *'I don't come on!'*

I hissed back, *'Yes you do. Come on!'*

'No, I don't come on here . . .'

'Come on!'

So she came on, and I said out loud, 'Wilson, would you take Flush out for a walk, please.'

She went to grab the dog, but Sally started running round and round the bed, and finally made her exit by leaping straight through the great blazing fire, the big, red, paper, stage fire. I'm afraid she got the biggest round of applause of the evening.

Our season in Llanelli was cut short early in the New Year when Dorothy Squires, who was a Llanelli girl, decided to buy the theatre and put on her own variety show. We were still playing when she had her bills pasted all over ours, saying, 'Dorothy Squires is coming to your local theatre.' We were a bit annoyed, to say the least. We had been doing very good business, and they often used to queue all the way round the theatre to get in to see us.

The International Players moved on to Gravesend. My digs there were with Mrs Bachelor, the best digs I have ever had. I'm not particularly interested in cooking, but I enjoy eating. When other people were learning to cook I was on stage acting, and getting home late at night to digs where the landlady would have a meal ready. Some of them were terrible, but Mrs Bachelor had been a professional cook. Cor! When we got in after the theatre, we could smell it. Three of us actresses – Mimi, Shauna and I – shared a basement flat, and she always cooked us something hot, and left it in the oven for when we got back from the theatre late at night. We used to get inside the front door and take a deep sniff to see if we could tell what it was, then we'd fly downstairs to eat it. She only charged us thirty bob a week. I don't know how she did it. Often in theatrical digs the more you paid the worse they were, because the nice, motherly landladies didn't like charging. I always shared digs with Mimi Gale. She became a very good friend, a lifelong friend. My daughters still call her 'Auntie' Mimi.

At Gravesend one week we were playing *The Perfect Woman*, and the perfect woman was a robot, played by Mimi. I was Auntie Goofy. They decided I needed padding, so I had this jacket made of cotton, stuffed with kapok. Mimi had to wear a sort of board, fixed over her head somehow, with all sorts of bobbins and wires. In one part of the play she goes berserk and knocks Auntie Goofy down, and lands on top. At rehearsal it was all right, but on the first night she knocked me down, landed on top, and couldn't get up because her wires had caught in my padding, and we were stuck together. I kept saying, 'Get up! Get up!' and she was saying, 'I can't! I can't!' The other actors had to lift us both up together and then separate us.

We went to Basingstoke next and did a short season there, and then we moved on to Sheerness in Kent for the summer season, and we were there for the whole of the summer from May to September, and in July I celebrated my twenty-second birthday there. Mimi and I found digs at Lil Dring's which we thought were not good, especially after Mrs Bachelor's, but I thought Sheerness itself was a lovely place, a Victorian terraced town on the end of nowhere, with a splendid promenade. The theatre was right opposite the sea, in the gardens. It was like a summer palace, made of glass. On warm summer evenings, once the theatre was full, they used to open up the sides so more people could come and watch, sitting in deckchairs on the lawns. They've taken the theatre down now. I went back not long ago, but it's all gone, and the whole town seemed forlorn and derelict. I have such happy memories of it as a beautiful, even a glamorous place, but the way of life has changed for ever for these old-fashioned seaside resorts. Perhaps, too, when I was young I was seeing it all through rose-tinted spectacles.

Gerald Harper joined the company at Sheerness. The producer said to me, 'We've got a young man coming who's just finished his RADA training. Would you mind coming in to audition with him?'

So I went in, and they gave him various things to read, and I read with him. Afterwards they said to me, 'What do you think?' and I said, 'Grab him!' So they did, and we spent the whole of that summer playing opposite each other. So I was Gerald Harper's first leading lady.

I liked Gerald immediately. He was very talented, enormously attractive and everything became great fun when he was around. I continued to take lots of character parts, but one week we were doing *While Parents Sleep*, and I was playing Lady Cattering, opposite Gerald. Lady Cattering carries on with all the men, so she's a 'wicked lady' part. She tries to seduce Gerald's character, and when we had the pensioners in for the matinee, they all used to shout, 'Oo! You bad 'un!'

I'd been doing quite a spate of funny old women before we did *While Parents Sleep*, and after the first night they wrote in the local paper, 'That old woman – she's not half bad when she's done up.' And there was I, looking forward to my twenty-second birthday in a few days' time! I just loved it.

After Sheerness we moved on to Paignton in Devon for the autumn of 1950. International Set, eh, what? Llanelli, Basingstoke, Gravesend, Sheerness and now Paignton . . . wow! Now that I was taking the leads so much of the time, I insisted on being given a rise to the princely sum of six pounds a week. That was my highest salary, six pounds, working as a professional actress before I gave it all up, because I had met the man I wanted to marry.

A certain John Staff lived in Llanelli. While I was there for the season from the autumn of 1949, I found a church to go to, St David's, where John was in the choir and I regularly saw him reading the lesson. He also ran the church youth club. There were two boys who were in the choir and in his youth club, who we all knew because they used to take part in our plays when young children were needed. In December they were in something, and their youth club were holding a Christmas party, and these two boys kept going on at us, trying to persuade members of the cast to come along. Finally a few of us younger ones, including Mimi and myself, decided that after the theatre we would look in on their Christmas party, which was fancy dress.

John Staff wasn't much of a dancer, so he preferred to be in charge of the cloakroom and hobnob from there. He had put his collar round back to front, and he had on one black and one brown shoe, because he was supposed to be an absent-minded vicar. But seeing the 'dog-collar' and not noticing his shoes, I thought he really was the curate, having so often seen him read the lesson.

As the party got going, one or two young fellows began to get a bit frisky. My friend Mimi enjoyed all that, but I retreated into the cloakroom and sat talking to John, who I still thought was the curate, only to discover that he was a student at Swansea University, reading pure mathematics. I always say he got me under false pretences. He told me it had caused quite a stir, the first Sunday I arrived at the church, because the boys who had been working in the theatre knew who I was, so there had been a lot of nudging and whispering along the choir, 'There's that actress from the Dock.' The theatre was actually called the Astoria, but the locals always called it the Dock.

So John knew I was an actress, but he had never been along to the theatre to see me in any of the plays, and he'd never spoken to me at church or taken any notice of me at all. At the end of the party he said, 'Do you know your way back to your digs?' and I said, 'No', because we'd gone straight to the party from the theatre, and the two boys had brought us, and I hadn't really noticed which way we'd come. So John walked Mimi and me home to our digs.

After that, every time I came out of the theatre at about quarter to ten at night, John would be there. He'd say, 'I've just been having a walk round . . .' Or he'd be on his bike, 'I was just having a bit of a ride round . . .' He just happened to be passing, that was all. I met his parents quite early on, because I went to his twenty-second birthday party on 1 January 1950. They didn't take to me at first. I think they were a bit afraid because I was an actress, and thought I was leading their son astray. I suppose you can understand it. This boy had always been so good and stayed quietly at home, and suddenly he was getting up and going out for walks and bike rides at ten o'clock at night. I suppose it's natural they were worried.

John was my first real boyfriend, although I was

too preoccupied with my life and work in the theatre to think of it as a romance. It was all quite down to earth on both sides. I suppose we were both rather serious characters, two young Christians who got on very well and agreed on many things. The company had to leave Llanelli not long after his twenty-second birthday, because of Dorothy Squires. We did have a quietly romantic evening together before I left. I think I knew that my feelings for him were stronger than anything I'd ever felt before, but it was not like Cathy and Heathcliff, nothing like that. We had only spent nine days together when we parted.

However, they do say that 'absence makes the heart grow fonder' and when I left Llanelli, it did. We used to write regularly, and found we agreed on so many things, and we met again the following summer at Sheerness, when John came down for three weeks' holiday. My parents and Con also came for one of the three weeks, so it was John's first meeting with my family.

Gerald Harper had joined the company by then. Gerald was very attractive, and I loved working with him, admired him, and was fond of him, but he always had an eye for the girls, so although I thought he was lovely, I knew too much about what he was up to.

When John arrived in Sheerness we soon realised our feelings for each other were serious, and the following Christmas, 1950, we were engaged. It's hard to describe how I felt. It was something that suddenly was part of me. I don't think we ever sat down and discussed getting married, it was just that gradually I couldn't imagine life without John. And I suppose he couldn't imagine life without me. So it was more that we became as one. I think this is the main thing – suddenly you are one person, and if anything happens to the other one, it's as though it's happening to you. This is how we became.

After his holiday at Sheerness, John graduated from university, and immediately joined the RAF to do his national service. In early 1951, he spent a weekend's leave in Dukinfield. It was quite a labour of love, a long journey up from RAF Yatesbury in Wiltshire. He went to Manchester, then he got on the Dukinfield bus, and I had told him to get off at the Chapel House, but the bus had gone past the town hall, up Chapel Street and on up Chapel Hill before he asked the conductor, 'Is this the Chapel House yet?' and was told, 'Oh no. You should have got off a mile back.' So he had to walk all the way back.

My mother and father thought he was absolutely wonderful. There was none of that 'not good enough for our girl'. He was, always has been, and still is a very genuine, kind, thoughtful, friendly man, and he was very good to my parents, who loved him dearly. As for me, well, I couldn't have done anything that I have done without his support, which he has always given me 100 per cent. He's the other half of me.

8

Married with Children

Although John's father, George Staff, was a tinplate
worker in Llanelli, neither of his parents were Welsh.
His father was from Bunwell in Norfolk originally,
and John's mother, Martha Mary, who everyone called
Polly, came from Felmersham, a lovely village in
Bedfordshire, where John's cousin, Paula, still lives,
with her husband, Chris, and their two children,
Victoria and Alex. John's mother had been in service
in Holland Park, London before the First World War.
George and Polly were married at St Barnabas' church,
West Kensington just after the First World War, and
soon afterwards they moved to South Wales, because
he had been injured in the war, and had been sent
to a hospital down there. He always walked with
two sticks.

They were elderly parents. John, their only child,
arrived late in their life, and was the apple of their eye.
He did very well at school and got a scholarship which
took him to a boys' public school, Llandovery College,
where he was a boarder. He did well academically and
became head boy. He went on to Swansea University,
which is where he was when we met, and planned to be
a maths teacher. They had invested everything in him,
their only son, and were immensely proud of him.

We had planned to marry in December 1951, a year after getting engaged and two years after our first meeting, but because John had been called up to do his two years' national service in the Air Force, where he would be earning very little money – ten shillings a week – John decided that we might as well at least claim the marriage allowance, so we brought the whole thing forward and got married in August 1951, on Ashton Wakes Saturday. The whole of Dukinfield used to close for the week of the Ashton Wakes. All the local business people and shops would take that week as a holiday, and everybody went to the fair at Ashton.

John's best man was Gwyn Evans, a friend from Swansea University who was also doing his national service in the RAF. Gwyn was cadging a lift in a plane up from Norfolk for the wedding. Because of high landing fees at Manchester Ringway, he landed at Hawarden, near Chester, and came on by train. It all took longer than he'd thought it would. We thought he'd got lost, because we'd heard nothing from him, and we had even arranged for my Uncle Harry to stand in as best man if he didn't arrive. But he finally turned up on the evening before. Con, who was to be my only bridesmaid, John and I were all down at St Mark's school where we were having the reception, getting all the place names and the tables ready so that only the food had to be brought in the next day.

Gwyn found us there, and we decided we should have some fun and go along to the Ashton Wakes. I used to love those fairground things, waltzing round on the moving carousel, so I took John on with me.

He has never been much of a dancer at the best of times, he sort of marches round, counting, so finding himself also spinning round and round, and up and down, it all proved too much for him. He came off absolutely green. I didn't know whether he'd be fit to walk down the aisle the next day, he was so sick.

We had one hundred people to our wedding, all the uncles and aunties and cousins as well as friends from round about, and Rev. Porter Tyson, our vicar and friend for eighteen years at St Mark's, came from his church at Mottram especially to marry us. I had the traditional, long, white wedding dress made of heavy silk brocade, with just a shoulder-length veil because I didn't fancy myself with a great, long, trailing veil. Con, my only bridesmaid, was dressed in very pretty pink silk, or silky satin.

In 1951, everything was still on ration, so feeding one hundred people was quite a tall order, but Uncle Clem got us tongue and sausage from his butcher's shop, and my mother prepared a lovely meal. There was dancing in the evening, and at nine o'clock John and I left them all still partying on, while we took a taxi down to Manchester, Piccadilly, or London Road as it then was, to go to London for our honeymoon. We had to change trains at Crewe around midnight. We had sandwiches with us, but some wag had put blotting paper in the top ones.

We arrived in London at four in the morning in pouring rain. We were staying at a hotel in Gower Street, and we couldn't get a taxi-driver to take us from Euston. They all said, 'It's only just round the corner.' So we walked, and by the time we reached our little honeymoon hotel on Gower Street, we were like two drowned rats. We had a little garret room, at the very top of the Regent House Hotel, opposite RADA. I had my photograph taken standing outside, and that's the nearest I ever got to RADA.

We went to the Festival of Britain on the South Bank, displaying all the country's achievements of the past one hundred years, since the Great Exhibition of 1851. There were no benches, and even the walls had been covered in sharp stones so you couldn't sit on them. John enjoyed the technical and science exhibitions rather more than I did. I got very tired. I liked the amusing 'World of Emmett' Clock further along the embankment, in the Festival Pleasure Park at Battersea, with funny people coming out of all the little doors every quarter of an hour, and the Emmett railway that took you all round Battersea Park. The evenings were the best time of all, when we went every night to the theatre. We saw the *Lyric Review for 1951*, with Dora Bryan being very comical. It was all a wonderful experience.

When we told his parents that we wanted to be married, John's father had said, 'Well, I think, John, you had better go to Manchester to find work. There will be better opportunities for you there than in South Wales.'

I was amazed. I hadn't expected that. I had been so sure they would want him to stay in Wales, to be near them. But now we could live in my old home ground, near my family and friends, and it was their own idea.

Then one day I got a telegram from them, not long before the wedding, saying, 'Sold the house. Find something.' They had decided to up sticks and come and live in Cheshire too, to be near John. They'd got a thousand pounds for their house in Llanelli, so that's what they had to spend. I got busy and found them a lovely big double-fronted Victorian house in Richmond Street, Ashton for just £950, because I managed to get the price knocked down a bit. That was quite an achievement, even in those days.

John was still away in the Air Force, and I was a bit upset when they insisted that I now go and live with them. I had been very happy, back at home staying with my parents, helping my mother with my father who still wasn't at all well, and preparing for the wedding. My mother had even bought a bed-settee for when John was able to come home at weekends. But suddenly I found myself living with people I didn't really know at all. John got married from their house, and then he had to go straight back in the Air Force, but I stayed on with them on my own. We certainly couldn't afford to buy or rent our own house, and they couldn't afford to keep such a big place going on their own. As it was a double-fronted house, they lived in one half and we had the other side.

It was rather a low time, I must say. I liked and respected John's parents, but somehow I could never feel comfortable or relaxed with them. They were really only interested in John, and I suppose they didn't quite know what to make of me. I was missing John, missing my family and missing the theatre. It was a complete change of life for me.

I decided to use my shorthand and typing skills again, to earn as much money as possible so we could save for a deposit on our own place. I couldn't have made nearly as much money by acting. My marriage allowance was only ten shillings, which even in those 'olden days', as our daughters will insist on calling them, was nothing really. So I went back to work as a secretary in an office in Manchester, at Richard, Johnson and Nephew. They were the biggest wire manufacturers in the country.

I was very afraid that when John eventually came back home, he would be quite happy for us to go on living in his parents' house. And at first it seemed that he was, so I was greatly relieved when only six months after he had been demobbed he said to me, 'We've got to have our own place.' I knew then that I'd married the right man.

He started his teaching career at Stockport Mile End Grammar School, only earning ten pounds a week, even as a qualified teacher with a degree, but within two years we had managed to save £155 in cash from my earnings, and we put it down as a deposit on a little 'semi' costing £1,550. In 1953, we moved into our first proper home of our own, 21 Hulme Road, Denton, about four miles from Dukinfield. John's parents sold the big house and moved into a smaller one. That was when we met Sheila and Jim Burton, who lived next door but one. We became inseparable, and until we had our children we were on holidays together. They are still our greatest friends.

I worked at Richard Johnson and Nephew for five years. I left in 1956, when I became pregnant. I was twenty-eight, which was considered quite late to be starting a family in those days, twenty-one or -two was thought to be the ideal. But with John's national service, we hadn't had much time together when we first married, and most of our courtship had been done through letters, because of my acting career; so now we wanted to be together for a year or two, just the two of us, in our own home, before starting a family.

It was to be a long period in the wilderness for me as far as acting was concerned. I produced shows for the church dramatic society, but I didn't perform. John and I always discuss everything before we make a decision, but I already knew in my own heart that the family would be the most important thing in my life, more important than any stage career, and I was going to give at least the first few years to bringing up our children, looking after them myself.

All this we had decided long before our first daughter, Katherine, was born. And, of course, when she did arrive, I loved her, and couldn't have handed her over to anyone else anyway. In a way she made life for us.

It was a difficult delivery. She was a breech baby, with extended legs. Instead of her head being at the bottom, her feet were, which made it very difficult, because they somehow had to get her out the wrong way round. Because it was a breach, I had to go into hospital the day before the baby was due. For the last few months of my pregnancy I hadn't been able to eat properly, just tiny snacks, because with the head high up, it pressed on my stomach. That first morning in hospital they brought me a boiled egg for my breakfast. I told them I couldn't possibly eat as much as that, but they said, 'Now, just you get that down you.'

The specialist came round as we were having breakfast. He examined me and said, 'I think your baby will probably be born this evening.' He'd only just left when I had to rush out to the toilet. I had terrible diarrhoea. I thought, 'They would make me eat that blooming boiled egg.' As I was washing myself down, I could feel something, and it was a tiny foot. I called the nurse, and you've never seen lights flashing or a trolley hurtling along a hospital corridor so quickly. They raced me to the delivery room, and the baby started to arrive as soon as we got there. They had to cut me open to get both feet out. But poor Katherine, and poor me, because her head, which is the big part, instead of pushing down and leading the way out had to be sort of pulled out. It was dreadful.

Katherine Ann was born on 21 December 1956, and by Christmas morning the pain was forgotten as I held the best Christmas present any mother ever gets, her newborn baby. John came to visit me in the evening, and after he'd kissed me, he said, 'How is the little boy?'

I said, 'It's a girl.'

He said, 'No, it isn't. They told me on the telephone. It's a boy.'

He went to find the Sister, and made her prove that it was a girl. He came back to me and said, 'Oh dear! I've sent dozens of cards out, saying it was a boy called Michael John.' So he had to send other cards out the next day saying 'Welcome to Katherine Ann'.

By 1958, I was expecting another baby. I kept saying to John, 'I'm sure this head is up here again.'

But the hospital insisted, 'Oh, no. You won't have a breech baby again.'

I was having exactly the same trouble with eating, and eventually they had to agree, this baby too was feet down. They took me in to hospital, gave me an anaesthetic and tried to turn her round, but she turned straight back again. So it was the same thing as with Katherine, and there was another terrible struggle to get her out. I had the gas and air, but they couldn't give me another anaesthetic, because I had to assist them. I could only push exactly when they were ready, because they were worried about the cord getting tied round the neck.

When poor Susan was born, she was black and blue from the waist down, because they'd bruised her so much, trying to turn her. They said afterwards it had probably happened because I have got such a big rib cage. So that's when we decided that two children was quite enough, and all we wanted.

Susan was born on 20 March 1959, an Easter baby, born in the penitential season of Lent, and Katherine was a Christmas baby, born in the penitential season of Advent.

Around the time Susan was born, my father started to have more of his agonising attacks, and once the police even came for me during the night to take me over to help. We didn't have a car in those days, so it was difficult for me to get down to see them, four miles away. Soon after Susan was born we moved back into Dukinfield, to a lovely Victorian house called Oaklands, at 6 Crescent Close, so that I could be on hand to help my mother.

It worked out well for everyone, because in 1958 John had moved school, to the maths department of Audenshaw Grammar School, and his parents' house was backing on to the school grounds, so he used to have lunch with them. They could see a lot more of him then, so they were very happy.

*   *   *

I've enjoyed every minute of my life, so I can't easily choose and say, 'This or that moment was the happiest time.' But I suppose, if I had to choose, it would be this period, when the children were small and my parents were still alive, and we were such a happy family then, very close, all working together. Sometimes my mother would go and pick the children up from school, or John would. The girls both went to St Mark's Infant and Junior School, where Connie and I had both gone, and where my father had gone. John usually finished teaching at 3.40 p.m., so when the children came out at 3.30 p.m, by the time they'd put their coats on and changed their shoes he could be there to pick them up if I or my mother couldn't.

We had many good friends in Dukinfield and at St Mark's church, where John and I, along with so many of my cousins and uncles and aunts, sang in the choir. I remember our two girls singing 'Vespers' one Sunday morning in church, when they were both very tiny. I'm not an emotional person – I like to keep my emotions in check – but I was near to tears then. These have been the taproots of my life: my family, my friends and my faith.

The reason my mother and John were sometimes picking up the girls from school for me was that Granada Television had recently come to Manchester, and from when Susan was a little over a year old, in 1960, I had begun, just two or three days a month, to do little bits of 'extra' work in television. After nearly ten years away from acting, I was getting back in the saddle again.

9

Extra Work

The telephone went one morning early in 1960, and a
familiar voice I hadn't heard for a while said, 'Why
aren't *you* down here?'

I said, 'Gerald! How lovely to hear your voice. What
do you mean? Down where?'

One of the first things they did at Granada Television
was a series called *Skyport*, and my old mate from the
International Players, Gerald Harper, had come up to
Manchester to play the duty officer. I hadn't been acting
at all for nearly ten years, but he and I had kept in touch.
He'd been to Manchester a few times, in *Seagulls over
Sorrento* and *Free as Air*, and we'd always gone to see
him and had a meal together.

'I'm at Granada Television, in *Manchester*. I thought
you'd have surely been here.'

'But I've got two little girls now.'

'Well, television isn't like the theatre, you know.
You do it during the day, when they're at school.'

I said, 'Really?' and he said, '*Yes*. Why don't you
come and get something?'

So I thought, 'Oh.'

Oldham Rep had always said to me, 'Whenever you
want work, you can come.' But it would have meant
that I would have had to be going out for the evening,

every evening, just when Katherine was coming home from school, and I didn't want that. This sounded different. I could just do little bits, the odd day, when Susan could stay with my mother for a few hours. I sat down and thought about it, and what I thought was, 'Oh, what a good idea.' I suddenly realised how much I had been missing my work as an actress.

George Bancroft, the boy from Blackpool who had been the student-actor with me in Aberdeenshire, was now working as an extra, and he told me about his agent, a Mrs E. V. Mullings, who he was sure would help me find work. So I went to see her, and she was wonderful, like having a 'mum' in the business. 'Mrs M' we all called her. She was married to Frank Mullings, an operatic tenor. He had died a long time ago when I went to her, but she used to talk about him as though he were still alive. She used to be a ballerina, and that was how they had met, in Sadler's Wells.

Mrs M had everybody on her books in those days, almost half the cast of *Coronation Street*, the new soap opera that came on the screen towards the end of 1960, were 'her' artists, including Pat Phoenix, Doris Speed, Bernard Youens, who played Stan Ogden, Brian Mosley and, I'm almost sure, Peter Adamson, who played Len Fairclough, and lots of others.

Mrs M immediately arranged for me to go and see someone at Granada, and someone at the BBC in Manchester, and they all said, 'We-ell. You've had a lot of experience in the theatre, but we would have to see you on camera. Would you be prepared to do some "extra" work to begin with?'

So I said, 'Yes. That's what I'm hoping for.'

It really was all I thought I was ever going to do

– little bits. So I did. I started as an extra, with non-speaking parts, walking on, or standing about in the background. *Skyport* was the very first 'walk-on' I ever did. It's all written down in John's Stockport School exercise book: '2 and 3 June 1960 – Granada – *Skyport*. Episode called: "The Meeting". Fee £6.'

Three pounds a day, that's what I used to get at the beginning. It was very good. They were a wonderful crowd of people doing extra work in those days, all professionals. Many's the time I've sat in the Rovers Return at a table with some of the best names from variety and repertory. Joan Heath and Penelope Davis were there. When I was a teenager and joined Oldham Rep, just to watch, they were the two leading ladies. Diana Davies, another very good actress who has been in *Emmerdale* recently, helped in the corner shop in *Coronation Street* for a time.

Before *Coronation Street* actually started, even the great Doris Speed was working as an extra. I used to have a red dress and a red coat with big wide sleeves and a big collar, and she used to say, 'Kathy, when you've finished with that coat, can I have it?' I often wondered, years later, when I had finished with it, whether she'd still want it. Annie Walker was to be her first big part on television, and as soon as the soap opera started, she became a star. She was a lovely actress. The other day I found an old letter from her in a drawer, and it quite touched me. She said, 'Your programme (*Last of the Summer Wine*) is going from strength to strength, but I'm sure they should realise that you are the strength.'

I had been pregnant with Susan in 1959 when they were originally casting *Coronation Street*, but if I had

had my choice and been there at the beginning, I'd have tried for the part of Ena Sharples, not Elsie Tanner. As it was, thanks to Mrs M, I've actually played ten different parts altogether in *Coronation Street*.

It was about a world I knew very well. In the early days, Ken Barlow's father had a hardware shop, and Ken was still a student. I'll tell you who else had a shop – my first two lines were in his shop – Mr Swindley, otherwise the incomparable Arthur Lowe. I was buying a jumper or a cardigan in Mr Swindley's shop for my mother. They used to call us extras 'speaking walk-on' if we had a line, or 'characterisation' if not. A characterisation didn't always get a name.

I was the Conservative candidate's wife at the council elections, when Len Fairclough put up to go on the council. I was Betty, a shop assistant. I was Mrs Thacker, a pensioner, complaining that they'd closed 'our' mission hall, and we'd had to go to that other mission hall, and she didn't like it one bit. It was draughty. Everything was wrong with it. So Mrs Thacker was a bit like a forerunner for Nora Batty.

The real forerunners to Nora Batty and the ladies' coffee mornings were, of course, Ena Sharples, Minnie Caldwell and Martha Longhurst, also known as Violet Carson, Margot Bryant and Lynne Carole, sitting round their little corner table, drinking stout in 'the snug' at the Rovers Return, while they put the world to rights. Woe betide anybody who tried to invade Ena Sharples' little domain in those days. When they were interviewing for the job of caretaker of the mission hall, I was a Mrs Helliwell, and I applied. But it was a put-up job, because Ena Sharples was always going to get it, and poor Mrs Helliwell never stood a chance. Everyone knew that.

The girls don't remember a time when I wasn't on television. I think it gave them a bit of status, rather than being teased, at school. Once, when Susan was very tiny, perhaps two, I was in *Coronation Street*, and she was sitting on my knee watching it, and it was one of the times when I had a couple of lines, and when I said the lines she said, 'Ooh! It talked!'

In 1962, Harry Worth was doing his series *Here's Harry*, at the BBC. I played one or two irate ladies for him. I always remember the funniest thing we did – well, I think so – he was in a call-box ringing America, and I was waiting for the telephone. He was putting all these sixpences in – you can imagine, can't you? to America? – he had one word and then it was 'Beep, beep, beep'. I'm waiting outside, looking black as thunder and knocking on the door. Later on we did a tour together. He was so funny with his lost, bemused face, and a really lovely man.

I was in so many programmes during the sixties, I can't remember them all. Granada did a series called *Mr Rose*, and I was in one episode as a prison wardress. I had to drag this woman, screaming, along to be hanged. Mrs M telephoned me immediately afterwards and said, 'I'm dreadfully sorry, Kathy. I wouldn't have let you do it if I'd known what they wanted you to do.'

'Oo,' I said, 'It was lovely!'

'Oh, no, it was awful. Awful!'

But I enjoyed it all so much, you see.

I was even briefly in an early *Crossroads* episode in 1971, as a completely different character from the part

I was later to become known for, Miss Doris Luke. In 1971 I was a Mrs Dingwall, arranging my daughter's wedding at the motel. I had scenes with Ronnie Allen, as the manager of the motel. My husband, Mr Dingwall, was played by Fred Feast – later to be Fred Gee who worked in the bar in *Coronation Street*.

The tenth and last part they ever gave me on the *Street* was a real character with her own story lines, Vera Hopkins. That was not until 1974, when I had already been playing Nora Batty for two years on *Summer Wine* – but that's another story. The very first appearance of Vera Hopkins was a nice one, because she had found out that her sixteen-year-old daughter, Trish (played by Kathy Jones), had been served in the pub. Vera was a really tough character, having a series of ding-dongs with Annie Walker across the counter at the Rovers. I enjoyed that.

After that, they kept calling any rather stupid, daft characters 'Vera Hopkins', so that I could play them. I got quite confused because one week Vera was on a committee interviewing people who wanted a job at the mission, I think it was, but a week or two later, she herself was applying for a job as a cleaner. I said, 'How on earth can this be the same person? It's only two weeks since I was on the committee.'

I wanted to say something to the director, but the producer's assistant took me on one side and said, 'Don't say anything. They've decided they like you, and they're going to write up this character for you. In the mean time they want this Vera Hopkins to just keep popping in here and there, now and then, to see if the audience like her. So just do what you can with her.'

I said, 'But that doesn't make my life any easier . . .'

Anyway, I did my best, and I suppose I must have done all right, because they did write her into the corner shop. Originally the corner shop had belonged to Florrie Lindly, played by Betty Alberge, who then sold it to Maggie Clegg, played by Irene Sutcliffe. Then Vera Hopkins and her family bought the shop from Maggie Clegg, and we all moved in.

When I'd first seen the name 'Vera Hopkins' on my script I had got quite excited. I said to them, 'Can I play it Welsh? With a name like Hopkins?' There was Jessie Evans – Jessie Éffans, talking like that – playing my mother-in-law, and Dicky Davis, the Welsh teacher in *Please Sir*, playing my husband. But they don't allow you, on television, to change your accent once you've been pigeonholed as a 'northern' actress.

'Oh no,' they said, 'your husband's Welsh, but you're northern.'

So that was a bit disappointing. Never mind, I enjoyed my time in the corner shop.

When I started out as an extra, I had never thought I would be doing anything much – only little bits and pieces – and when we had insurance cards it was such a nuisance if your married name was different from the card, so it was easier if I didn't use my old stage name, Katherine Brant, but started work again as Katherine Staff. Gerald Harper always said I had 'a following round the country' as Katherine Brant, and that I shouldn't change it, but I said, 'Oh well, I'll only be doing little bits.' Later on Mrs M decided to change it further, because she said, 'Every time we get a good part, the contract comes made out to "Kathy". There must be some reason there. Perhaps Katherine is too long.' So we changed it officially to Kathy Staff, and that's who I've been ever since. My sister Con never likes it. She thinks I should still be Katherine Brant, but only because she helped me to choose it, I think.

Meanwhile, Gerald Harper had become a big star on television. I always knew he had something special, from when I first heard him read at Sheerness. To play a cad, you can't beat him, but he could also play a lovely, gentlemanly character like Hadleigh, the local squire, and before that he'd been Adam Adamant – a very attractive character. When he started doing *Hadleigh*, they cast me as his housekeeper. I was so excited. I went down to London, and he came in, the big television star, chatting graciously to people. I was sitting waiting with my coffee when he suddenly saw me, and he just roared with delight and gave me such a big hug. Unfortunately I was only in two episodes. His character got married, so they didn't need a housekeeper any more, which was a bit of a blow.

That's how I started in television, and it was Gerald who got me going. Whenever I see him, he always reminds me of that. We kept in touch for years, then it got to just Christmas cards, then he moved and we moved, and you know how it is.

I was quite content all through the sixties, and never thought of doing anything more. We had a car by then, so I used to drive down to Manchester. It only took me twenty-five minutes to get down to Granada or the BBC from Dukinfield. I had a good husband, the two girls and a nice home. It was a very happy time. And God was so good, because when the girls were small, that was all I did, bits and bobs and walk-ons. My first real break didn't come until they were older. In 1969, my first major television role came along, playing with Roy Barraclough in a soap opera called *Castle Haven*, two episodes a week, and by then Susan was ten and Katherine was twelve.

Everything I did in those early days is written down in John's exercise book. My first year's work only took up two pages, and the second year's work was only a bit longer. My entire early television career for the first nine or ten years is recorded in one Stockport School exercise book. Entries like: '10 June 1963: *Coronation Street*, ten guineas for two days.' (It must have gone up from three pounds.) '1966: *Coronation Street* repeats – 2 × 40 per cent of seven guineas.' We didn't even bother to go into hardback until the seventies, when he started using Audenshaw Grammar School exercise books.

10

The Everetts and the Desponds

I first met Roy Barraclough one day in 1969, when we found ourselves both going for the casting interviews for *Castle Haven*, a new soap opera being made by Yorkshire Television. Roy had been a leading actor at Oldham Rep for a few years, and I had seen him give many good performances, but we had never met. Roy lived at Oldham, so we had both got on the train at Manchester.

We liked one another right from the start, and have always got on well. We discovered that we had a lot in common, thought alike about many things, and we immediately became – and have remained – really good mates. We even share the same birthday.

We both got the parts we read for in *Castle Haven*, so from then on we travelled every day to Yorkshire Television together, taking the Trans-Pennine Express from Stalybridge to Leeds, rehearsing all day, and catching the train back at about five o'clock, so I was always home in time to give the children their tea and put them to bed.

Castle Haven was about an old house that had been turned into flats. The house that it is supposed to be about is at Whitby, the one with a conical roof, just below the whale bone motif overlooking the harbour.

The cast didn't ever actually go there, because we did everything in the studios at Leeds, but the crew went to Whitby to film the outside of the house that was supposed to be Castle Haven.

It went out twice a week, and the stories were about all the different types of people who lived in the various flats. We had Gretchen Franklyn and George Waring playing the caretakers in charge, who lived in the basement. Then there was a young schoolteacher and his wife, newly-weds, played by Sally James and Jack Carr, so their flat was modern and had all new things from their wedding present list. There was an old couple, played by the excellent Bert Palmer and Nathalie Kent. They had everything very old-fashioned in their flat, all their old knick-knacks. One of my greatest friends in the theatre is an Austrian actor, Ernst Valder, who some people will still remember as Ivan Chevesky, Elsie Tanner's son-in-law, when *Coronation Street* first started. Ernst came into *Castle Haven*, playing Dr Josif Pospichal, and because he'd been in the *Street*, he was treated more like 'a star' than the rest of us. He's gone back to Austria now, but we keep in touch and he comes over here every year for a holiday. Jill Summers and Ann Way owned the pub called the Lighthouse, and later Jill was to be in *Coronation Street* as Phyllis until she died a few months ago.

There must be thousands of budding actors and actresses who never make it to the top of their profession. It's a shame, because many of them are so good, and you just don't understand why some people are successful and others aren't. Jan Davies, who was Mrs Pike in *Dad's Army*, was in *Castle Haven* for a time, which is how I met her. She became a very dear friend, and she was a lovely actress who never really got as much work or the parts she deserved. I was devastated when she died of lung cancer a few years ago.

The best parts in comedy always seem to be written for men – certainly this used to be so. Now, why is this? *Dad's Army* was mainly men, *Only Fools and Horses* was mainly the men, and even where there are parts for women, like in *Men Behaving Badly* or even my own *Last of the Summer Wine*, it's still the men who get by far the biggest share of the storylines. I suppose it's getting a little better, but it's still very hard for many a comedy actress to find enough work to keep herself fully employed.

Back to *Castle Haven* – Roy Barraclough and I were the Everetts, Harry and Lorna, with two children, Sylvia and Dickie (played by Sharon Campbell and Alan Guy), and we were the poor, feckless ones, who lived in a tatty, untidy flat. We were always having money problems and couldn't pay our rent.

Birmingham's ATV wouldn't take *Castle Haven* because of *Crossroads*. Manchester's Granada wouldn't take it because of *Coronation Street* and London's Thames Television wouldn't take it because they said there were too many soaps already. It was shown all the way down the Yorkshire coast, Southern had it, Wales had it, Scotland had it, but none of the major ITV companies. They were hoping all the time to get a breakthrough. If just one of the big companies would have taken it, they would have kept it on. But none of them would, so it only ran for thirteen months, between 1969 and 1970.

*   *   *

I met the remarkable Jess Yates while I was working at Yorkshire, 'the bishop', as they called him. He did wonders for Yorkshire Television, absolute wonders. He got stars there for *Junior Showtime* and *Stars on Sunday*, big stars, and paid them next to nothing. He'd have them there all day, and persuade them to perform number after number. Some of them would nearly collapse by the end of the day. When we were doing *Castle Haven*, the girl playing our daughter was actually a singer, Sharon Campbell, and she was only sixteen. Jess Yates had this idea that he would have her on *Junior Showtime*, and of getting Roy and me to sit in the audience, watching her doing her number. So we said, 'What do you mean, Jess? As ourselves?'

'No, no. You'll be Harry and Lorna Everett.'

So we told our agents and, of course, they asked for a fee. Jess nearly went spare. We said, 'But you're asking us to dress up, make up, do a performance.'

He said, 'Well! I was going to give you a jelly tea.'

And that's all he ever gave those children who took part, with all those episodes – a jelly tea. We declined.

He was destroyed in the end. I don't think he deserved as much as he got. I think it was a vendetta, but I don't know why. I always got on very well with him, but he certainly was a hard man. I remember going in the canteen one day, and he called me over, 'Kathy, come and say "hallo" to our Gracie.' I could hardly believe it. The fabulous Gracie Fields was sitting there, and I sat with them in the canteen. It was such a thrill for me to meet her, but she looked exhausted. After a bit Jess said, 'Well, come on, Gracie, if you'll just do a couple more numbers . . .'

She was so frail and old by then, and she looked at him and said weakly, 'Oh! I can't do any more. I've done eight songs. I can't sing any more. I've no voice left.'

He winked across at me, and said to her, 'All right, darling. All right. Come back next week, and we'll do these other two.'

She was almost crying, 'But I can't come back next week . . . Oh, all right then. Come on,' and stalked out.

I thought, 'You rotter!' but he got his ten songs out of Gracie.

Straight after *Castle Haven* ended in 1970 I went in as a 'visiting star' for two plays at Oldham Rep: *The Corn is Green*, immediately followed by *Friends and Neighbours*. So at long last I had achieved my childhood ambition of playing Oldham Rep – I could say that I had really made it.

Over the next few years Roy Barraclough and I both worked regularly with Les Dawson, who had seen us together in *Castle Haven*. He first asked us to do a little half-hour play with him for his series, *Dawson's Weekly*, where we were the family waiting for the will to be read, and I was Auntie Minnie – funnily enough. The whole family had 'great expectations', but of course, in the end, it was the young layabout played by Les Dawson who got all the money.

Much later, in 1975, when Les was doing a *Les Dawson Spectacular*, he asked me to go on. I'd never done 'variety' on television before. I went to Yorkshire Television, and they said, 'You're in Dressing-room 2.' I knew the place so well, having worked there for so long on *Castle Haven*, and I thought, 'Coo! Going up in the world! That's a very big dressing-room.' Then I went in, and there were all these costumes hanging up. Every rail was full. I thought, 'I must be sharing it with a lot of people.'

There were actually six full period costumes – and they were all for me. Les was playing Henry VIII in a sketch, and I was to play all six of his wives. I spent more time in wardrobe, putting on different costumes and being made up, than I did saying the lines. It was all, 'She's for the chop!' and off I'd go again to change into my next costume.

In 1976, when he was doing *Sez Les*, Les asked Roy to go in and do 'Sissy and Ada' with him, originally just a one-off, the two of them dressing up as women, and doing it virtually ad lib, without a script. That's when they first invented it. Later on he asked me to go into *Sez Les* with them, and once again I was to play *all* the women's parts, whether it was a young secretary, his wife, an old battle-axe hitting him with an umbrella – whatever the role was, if it was female, I played it. We had Alvin Stardust in as a guest star once, I remember. I was dressed as a terrible, toothless old crone with a big umbrella, and had to go in screaming, 'Alvin! Alvin!' and hitting Les Dawson with the umbrella, saying, 'Get out of the way.' Another time I was a gangster's moll, with a beauty spot, smoking cigarettes.

In all, I did four series of *Sez Les* during the seventies, acting in hundreds of different sketches. My favourites were when we were the Desponds, a miserable family. It was black humour, ahead of its time. Les was Mr Despond, I was Mrs Despond, Roy was the lodger, and Norman Chappell was Grandad.

The front-door bell used to play the 'Dead March' from *Saul*. The Desponds were always being interviewed by Julian Orchard, of the BBC, and the family kept saying that everything was 'Terrible. Terrible!'

Then there was 'The Desponds in Concert'. We were all at a concert, and they cut to us sitting in the audience looking miserable, saying, 'This is terrible. I mean, we could do better.' So they say, 'Would you like to come down and try?' Imagine Les Dawson, Roy Barraclough and myself, standing there in a forlorn row singing, 'Happy talking, talking happy talk' with long, miserable faces. It was a scream. Les wrote that sketch himself, but he had a lot of excellent people like Barry Cryer writing material for him. We had another one with the Desponds visiting somebody in hospital. There was this poor man, with us three miserable people sitting looking at him, and we interfered with the pulley holding his leg, making it shoot up in the air.

It was fantastic, working with Les. At the end of rehearsals he would get on the piano and start playing, you know how he did, all wrong, and we'd say, 'Please, Les. Don't. Don't! We can't stand any more.' Because we just laughed until we were aching. All day we laughed, and I'd be thinking to myself, 'And I'm being paid for this!'

What a sad day, when he died in 1993. His wife, Tracy, had taken him to the hospital in Manchester just for a check-up, because he'd had heart trouble before, but this time the doctor checked him and said, 'Oh yes. Great. You're fine. Everything's OK.' So then Tracy said to Les, who was still lying on the bed, 'Would you like a cup of coffee before we drive back home?'

and he said, 'Yeah.' I suppose she could have pressed a bell and asked them to bring them two coffees, but instead she went down to get it herself, and when she came back she thought that he'd fallen asleep, so she just put his cup down for him, and drank hers. She told me later, 'He was still sitting up in bed, quite peaceful, just as he had been, but his eyes were closed. And then I suddenly realised – he wasn't there.'

The Theatrical Comedy Association have put a blue plaque on his house in St Anne's, a beautiful house he bought before the property boom in the seventies, when we were all working on *Sez Les* together, and it's where Tracy and their daughter Charlotte still live. Roy unveiled the plaque, and there were so many stars there. Tracy sends us a photograph every year of their 'little Charlotte'. I always look forward to receiving the photographs, and seeing her growing up. She can play the piano like her Dad. She's got a funny look of him. Maybe she'll be a talented comedian, like her Dad. That would be great.

Back to the beginning of the seventies, after *Castle Haven* had come to an end, Kevin LeFann, who had written *Castle Haven*, went straight on to set up *Emmerdale Farm*, or *The Sugdens* as they were going to call it at first. I auditioned, and they had got it down to two of us to play Annie Sugden, but then I got a letter saying they were sorry, but they felt I was too young for the part. Freddie Pine was playing the son, and he was my age. So Sheila Mercier played Annie. Ah, well. That's show business. If I'd have got it, there'd have been no Nora Batty, or not for me. John has the famous entry in his school book: '5 June 1972: interview at BBC Peter House for *Comedy Playhouse: Last of the Summer Wine.*'

11

Is it . . . Nora?

As you will have guessed by now, my mother's kind
efforts to prevent everybody calling me Nora, by
christening me Minnie instead of Leonora, proved
to be in vain, because nowadays so many people
do call me Nora. If Thora, Dame Thora Hird, who
I've admired for as long as I can remember, hadn't
called her own recent volume of autobiography, *Is it
Thora?* I might well have thought of calling mine *Is it
Nora?*, because I'd be a very rich woman if I could
have a pound for every time someone has come up
to me and asked that.

I had absolutely no idea, at the beginning, how big it
would be. It was 1972. We had just got home from
holiday. John, Katherine, Susan and I had been to
Benidorm, with my cousin Frances and her two
children, and we arrived home in the early hours
of 5 June. John drove us back from Heathrow, and
then we all went straight to bed.

I didn't wake up until about twelve o'clock. I had
just put all the washing in the machine when the
telephone rang. It was Mrs M, my agent, saying, 'The
BBC are doing a new series of *Comedy Playhouse* and
they'd like to see you – today.'

I said, 'Oh no, Mrs M. I'm not going all the way back down to London now. We only got home in the early hours this morning.'

But she said, 'No, no. You won't have to. They're seeing people up here, in Manchester.'

So I said, 'Oh. Oh well, then, if they can give me a late appointment, I suppose I could go and see.'

She called me back a bit later and said, 'They say, "Would four o'clock be late enough?" That's their last appointment.'

'Oh, I suppose so,' I said. It didn't seem very important.

I did put on a rather smart black velvet trouser suit, because you always want to make a good impression, and drove myself down to Peter House in Manchester. I went in, and was taken straight in to see Jimmy Gilbert, then head of comedy at the BBC. I hoped I was looking quite good, tanned, trim and tiptop after my holiday, so I remember I was a bit taken aback when he took one look at me and said, 'Oh dear me, no. I'm sorry. You're nothing like the part we're looking for.'

I said, 'Oh, thank you very much.'

He said, 'I am sorry. Have you travelled far?'

I said, 'Well, seven miles.'

'Oh well, I suppose now you're here, you may as well read it, but you're nothing like the part we're looking for.'

He handed me a script, and I had to read the first line in the first scene of a half-hour play called *Last of the Summer Wine*. It was written by Roy Clarke, and was one of six new half-hour comedies the BBC had commissioned as 'pilots'. If any one of them were any good, they were going to do a series later.

The scene I had to do for my audition was the camera panning round, coming to a halt on me hanging out my washing, whereupon I say to another neighbour, hanging out her washing, 'They're tecking his tele again.'

Then the camera pans round to the door under Nora Batty's steps, and two men appear, carrying a television set. Then Bill Owen, as Compo, comes out and says, 'Whoor! Mrs Batty!' and I cover up my bloomers on the washing-line with a towel.

That was it. It was the first line and the first scene of the first ever episode of *Last of the Summer Wine.* It came quite automatically to me, how to do it. I'd known so many women like that, who kept an eye on the goings-on in the town. When I was little I used to see them use a donkey stone to clean their front doorsteps. They'd wet the flags, rub them all over with the sand-coloured block of donkey stone, then they'd use a cloth to smooth it over. It coloured the flagstones, making them look nice and creamy. Some of the women, who were all very house-proud, used to even clean the paving-stones on the road in front of their house as well. And woe betide anyone who dared to walk over *their* paving-stones when they'd just done it . . . A real Nora Batty would come out shouting, 'What do you think you're doing? Get off!'

So I knew all about those sort of women, and I knew exactly how to do it. I was quite relaxed about auditioning the scene, because as Jimmy Gilbert had said, 'You're nothing like the part.' Why worry? He and I played the scene.

As soon as I'd finished he exclaimed, 'That's it! That's her! But we were looking for a really big, fat woman, because we don't know whether or not this scruffy, dirty little man *really* fancies her, or if she's so dreadful *nobody* could fancy her.'

After twenty-five years, we still don't know, do we, whether Compo really fancies Nora, or whether it's all a big leg-pull? That's Roy Clarke's clever writing. If they settled it once and for all, you'd have nowhere to go.

They gave me the part, as I suppose you know, and asked me to wear padding, and to make myself look as fat and as unlikely a sex object as possible. So that's how poor Nora Batty was born. And of course, after the pilot, we did the series.

The popularity of the series built up gradually. I remember someone writing in a newspaper that they wanted to keep it secret how good it was in case 'they' spoilt it if it became too popular. Then in the mid-seventies, there was an ITV strike. I think until then a lot of people had assumed that there was nothing very entertaining to watch on BBC, and preferred ITV for comedy programmes. They all switched over during the ITV strike, and saw *Summer Wine* for the first time, and we rocketed to the top of the ratings. We got absolutely huge audiences, and they stayed with us, even after the strike was over. That was our heyday, the mid- to late seventies.

One Monday morning in the late seventies, I was travelling by train from Stockport to Birmingham to do *Crossroads*. The man sitting opposite me was reading his *Daily Star*, and it said on the front page, 'I Love Nora Batty Week – get your sticker.' It was a very queer sensation, sitting there, reading this. When I got to Birmingham, I rang John and said, 'It's "I Love Nora Batty Week" in the *Star*. Go and get a paper and a sticker and see what it's all about.' They'd sold out in Dukinfield, so he went down to the offices in Manchester where they said, 'Sorry, they've all gone. But we'll be getting some more, because it's running all week.' It really did feel strange, a whole week of articles all about Nora, and you could get car stickers saying 'I love Nora Batty.' I've still got mine.

Often articles that appear about me in the papers will say, 'She is nothing like Nora Batty', but if I'm honest, we do have some things in common. Like Nora, I am a strong, northern lady from the working classes. We've seen Nora organising jumble sales for the church, trying to get people for the concert at the church, cleaning the church, so she's obviously a committed Christian, and so am I. And her home, Holmfirth itself, is no more than twenty minutes' drive from the area where I have lived for most of my life, and still live.

Roy Clarke had originally thought of Rotherham as the setting, and he took Jimmy Gilbert to look at it from the hills above it, but he'd said, 'No. It's far too big.' It was Barry Took, who had recently made a documentary there about the changelessness of places like Holmfirth, who suggested it. Neither Roy nor Jimmy had ever heard of it, but they went to look and as soon as they saw it they both said at once, 'Yes! This is the place.'

I *hope* I've got a better sense of humour than Nora, because she's a bit dour, and everything is very serious to her, whereas I do try to see the funny side of things. You're always laughing *at* Nora rather than with her. She can't possibly have much of a sense of humour, otherwise she'd laugh at some of Compo's antics instead of always hitting him with her broom. She's like a battered old trout who can't stop itself from rising each time to Compo's fly. She's an archetype of perpetual innocence. Although she's a gossip, and she likes to lay down the law, she somehow never sees what Compo is up to. They always show a close-up of her face a few seconds before she is going to be set upon by Compo. It's a study of puzzlement and bewilderment. Everyone knows what's going to happen. Compo, Clegg and Foggy know, the audience knows; only Nora has no idea. That's why she's funny.

As you now know, as Nora Batty I wear padding, but every year we get different people responsible for make-up and wardrobe. They ring me up and ask what make-up I have for Nora, and I say, 'No make-up, just broken veins on my nose and cheeks, no lipstick, hair-curlers and heavy eyebrows.' And that's it. I'm made to look terrible. When I started, they even put bags under the eyes to make me look older.

One year, a girl rang up and said she was the costume designer for that year's series. She said, 'Now I wonder if you could come to London, because I'd like to buy some new clothes for Nora.'

I said, 'Well, that's very kind of you, but really there's no point in my coming, because I wear padding as Nora Batty. What they usually do is to go out and buy a size twenty-two or twenty-four dress or coat, and that'll fit over Nora Batty's padding.'

'Oh. Right.' Then, just as I was putting the telephone down, she said, 'Well, in that case, if you have any of your own clothes which would be suitable, would you just bring them along?'

There was no answer to that.

I don't dress anything like Nora, I should hope.

I wear trouser suits quite a lot. I wear long skirts, never minis, and enjoy looking smart in good designer clothes. Only last week a lady offered to send me a load of funny old-fashioned hats she said she had left over from the sixties, as though I walked around in terrible hats like Nora Batty's all the time. I do wear hats for very smart occasions, when I think a woman needs a hat to finish off her outfit, but unlike Nora, I know how to wear mine the right way round.

Alike or different, I never bring her home with me. I don't believe so much in the characters I play that I think they really exist. It's just this scene and that scene. Nora Batty doesn't exist. Nora Batty is just a pile of padding, curlers, pinny and wrinkled stockings on the floor of the dressing-room when I leave the set of *Summer Wine*. There's got to be some of you in each part you play, in that it comes from inside. But it's my work. I never bring it home, apart from struggling to learn my lines for the following day.

My John has always found *Last of the Summer Wine* very funny. It's just his sense of humour. I like it too, but I sometimes think it appeals even more to men than to women. John used to come along to the studios sometimes, to watch the recordings. Once or twice he has laughed so loud and been too near a microphone, so he has been asked to move further away.

Unfortunately there was one person who never liked seeing me as Nora Batty – my Mum. She often used to say, 'I don't like you working with those dirty old men.'

I would say, 'They're not really dirty old men. They're just acting.'

'Oh yes, they are. I can tell.'

'Well, I'm not really like Nora Batty, am I?'

'That's different.'

12

Mum

With so many members of the family around, living in or near Dukinfield, I don't think my mother often suffered from loneliness after my father died, but of course life was never the same. She had kept him going for sixteen years after the war, and now there was no one who depended on her as much as he had. She must have missed him badly, but I don't think she was unhappy. She had her grandchildren, Con's two daughters, Alison and Helen, and our two daughters, Katherine and Susan, who she loved dearly, and all her own and my father's brothers and sisters, and all their families. We've all always been very close, so she was never alone. She was part of the 'family choir' at St Mark's, Dukinfield, and as long as she had music, she was happy.

Then in 1976 she had to have an operation for cataracts. I don't know what happened, but it went wrong, and afterwards her sight grew worse and worse, until she could hardly see. She told me that it was taking her twenty minutes to get downstairs. I think that somehow during the operation they may also have touched her brain, because from then on she started to become very confused.

We became seriously worried about her having a

fall down the stairs. Con lived in Yorkshire, and it would have been hard for Mum to move so far away from Dukinfield, the home-town she'd known all her life, but I was working away so often, I didn't think it would be easy to have her coming to live with us either. But we did try. In 1973 John and I had moved a few miles away from Dukinfield, to Mottram in the Longdendale valley, where the artist L. S. Lowry spent the last years of his life. Mottram was a pretty, rural village in those days, with an old church with a spire, but still within easy reach of Manchester, and in 1973 they were building some new houses there. It was somewhere I'd always fancied living. We had been having a lot of trouble and expense with the roof of our old Victorian house in Dukinfield, so we decided that we would move, and buy one of these modern houses.

In 1976 my mother came to stay with us, but she didn't seem to know where she was. John and I went out to do the shopping one day, and left her sitting by the fire. We were only out for half an hour, but when we got back the neighbours were round. She'd decided she wanted the fire higher, but when she'd turned the knob, it had gone off, and then she didn't know whether the gas was still coming out, so she'd gone running out in a panic to the neighbours. When it was bedtime she'd start putting her coat on. I'd say, 'But you're staying here with us now, Mum.'

She'd say, 'No, I'm not, I'm going to my home. I'm not staying here.'

It was very difficult. In the end we all agreed that it would be better if she went back to Dukinfield, where everyone and everything was familiar, but that she should move into sheltered accommodation. She went to live at Fir Trees, a big nursing home in Dukinfield. There she had a pleasant bed-sit, with her own little kitchen off the room, but quite soon she couldn't even make herself a cup of tea, because she couldn't see to pour the water. It was terribly sad. She went down hill so quickly after the cataract operation. Every day she got more and more confused.

She didn't know me one day. I called in one afternoon, and she was up and dressed, but I could see she wasn't well so I made her a cup of tea and helped her to get back into bed. In the evening, the girls and John had a dramatic society meeting, so I said, 'I think I'll pop in and see if Mum's all right.'

They dropped me off at her door, and when I went in she was up again, sitting in her chair. I said, 'I thought you weren't feeling very well, and were staying in bed today.'

She said, 'Who are you?'

I said, 'It's me. Minnie.'

'Oh no, you're not. I don't know who you are.'

She really didn't know me. I rang my sister and said, 'Will you tell her who I am, Con.'

Con tried, but she couldn't get her to understand over the telephone. That is an awful thing, when your mother doesn't know who you are. It broke my heart. I didn't know what to do. She wouldn't let me put her back to bed. She said, 'No. You can't do that. No, no, no. They'll come and attend to me soon.'

I said, 'John will be here soon.'

She seemed very surprised and pleased. She said, 'Have *you* got a John, too? I've got a John. He's so good to me.'

And when John arrived, she was all right with him. She knew him. We got her back into bed between us.

She continued to deteriorate, and that Christmas, when we were out carol singing, I said, 'There's a light on in Mum's flat. We'd better go and see.'

We went in, and they told us she'd fallen out of bed on to the floor. She'd had a stroke. I stayed the night, and from then I stayed with her virtually all the time. My sister, who was teaching, came over at weekends.

By 2 January she had become unconscious. She was making a terrible noise all the time, with her breathing. The doctor said he thought she wouldn't come out of the coma, and it could be an hour or a week, but it wouldn't be long before she died. That Sunday evening, John and the girls had gone to church, and I was sitting there, listening to this terrible noise her breathing made, which had been upsetting me so much I hadn't been able to sleep for a couple of nights. I thought I'd turn the television on, so that at least I wouldn't be able to hear it so much. It was *Songs of Praise* from Blackburn Cathedral, and choirs from all over Lancashire were singing, 'O Jesus, I have promised to serve thee to the end,' and I joined in. While I was singing, I realised the noise had stopped. She was breathing normally. I carried on to the end of the hymn, and she opened her eyes and said, 'That was lovely.'

She had a little tea, and when John arrived, with flowers from church, she said, 'Oh, those are lovely.' She could see them and smell them, and it was like magic. She had always said, 'Music will bring me back, if anything will.' She had been in a coma for days, and the music had brought her back. It was the love of her life, singing and music. But later on that night she slipped back into unconsciousness again.

It was still the school Christmas holidays, so the next day, Monday, my sister came over from Yorkshire and said, 'You go home now and get some sleep.' Mum was still unconscious, so I did go home. I'd only had an hour's sleep when the telephone rang, and they said, 'Will you get back, we think your mother's dying.' She had already gone by the time I got there.

It was very sad, but she wouldn't have wanted to carry on, losing her senses more and more. I'm very glad I was there when she came back to us for that little while and was her old self; and that Con had been with her at the end, so she hadn't been alone.

Mum died in January 1977. As she had never really enjoyed seeing me as Nora, I've always felt it was a shame that she never saw me in *Crossroads*. In 1978, I went into *Crossroads* to play Miss Luke, and I know she would have loved Doris Luke, a strong woman who was also kind and gentle – very similar, in fact, to my mother, who was a very strong woman, but oh, with a heart of gold.

13

Crossroads

I don't deliberately base parts on real people, least of all myself. I 'see' the character in the lines, and it comes to life. But sometimes with Miss Luke, I used to watch myself, and I could see my mother. At other times I could see my Auntie Alice, my dad's sister, who I also resembled. For that reason I never really liked watching myself on *Crossroads*. I enjoy watching *Summer Wine*, because it's my sense of humour, but my character in *Crossroads* was just a bit too close to home for comfort. It wasn't a deliberate decision on my part. Doris Luke just happened to have been written as a character who was very like two women I was very close to.

In 1978 ATV telephoned to ask me to do thirteen weeks as Doris Luke, a new character on *Crossroads*, but I saw immediately that the dates we were filming that year's *Last of the Summer Wine* Christmas Special would come right in the middle of it. Sydney Lotterby, the producer of *Summer Wine*, was on holiday, but fortunately he'd given me his home telephone number, so I called him and told him the problem. 'Oh, don't worry,' he said. 'Tell Jack Barton (the producer of *Crossroads*) to ring me, and we'll sort out something.'

They did arrange it between them, and for one

frenzied week I was doing both. I worked on *Crossroads* on Monday and Tuesday in Birmingham. Then on Wednesday I went to the BBC in London and blocked *Summer Wine* and rehearsed it the following morning. Then back up to Birmingham to record the episodes of *Crossroads* on Friday.

On Saturday, I had to rush straight back down to London to rehearse *Summer Wine* in the studios all afternoon. On Sunday we did a final run-through of *Summer Wine*, had our dress-rehearsal, and then recorded it in front of an audience. On Sunday night, I travelled back up to Birmingham and started again on *Crossroads* on Monday morning.

The producer of *Crossroads*, Jack Barton, asked if I would work for eighteen weeks, long before I'd completed the thirteen weeks I was booked for. This is what they used to do in *Crossroads*. You'd go in for a particular storyline, and however many weeks that story lasted, that was how long you were contracted for. But if the writer wanted to take the character on into the next story, your contract was extended. I'd only done a couple more weeks into the eighteen, when Jack Barton asked me if I would become a 'regular'. I said, 'Well, I do have *Summer Wine* to do every year.'

He said, 'If you give us three months' notice, we'll write you out for however long you need to do your *Summer Wine*, and then you'll come back to us.'

For the next seven years, I worked for nine months on *Crossroads* and for three months on *Summer Wine*. Miss Luke had various 'accidents' to explain her frequent absences, and it was a bit embarrassing because I used to get so many 'get well' cards, and you can't really write back and say, 'You silly old thing. I'm doing *Summer Wine*.' Instead I used to wait until I was going back into *Crossroads* and then write and say, 'Thank you so much for your card. I'm so much better and will soon be back at the Crossroads Motel.' Oh dear!

Terry Wogan was the first one to tumble to it. I had been doing *Crossroads* and *Summer Wine* for a year, and one day, he suddenly said on his morning radio programme, 'Do you know? I think Nora Batty is Doris Luke's sister!'

I thought, 'Oh yes – here we go.'

After that, nearly every morning, it was something about either Nora or Doris. He did a lot for my publicity, I must say. Terry even gave me a saucy suspender-belt, to keep my wrinkled stockings up. I was doing an interview with Gloria Hunniford one lunchtime on Radio 2, and he'd been in the studio in the morning. He left a midnight-blue suspender-belt dangling round the clock for when I arrived.

Then he started saying on the programme, 'Nora Batty is going to "streak" at the Rugby League Cup Final.'

He kept going on about whether she would or not. Lo and behold, two tickets came for John and me for the cup final – and who do you suppose we were sitting next to? Terry kept saying, 'Oh, go on, Kathy. Go on. Do a streak.'

I said, 'I'll chase *you*. If you streak – I'll come after.'

Meanwhile, I continued to do the two series, *Summer Wine* and *Crossroads* side by side every year. There wasn't a lot of time for holidays for the years between 1978 and 1985. In 1981 I even managed to do a series as Mrs Blewitt in *Open All Hours* with Ronnie Barker as well. I must admit, Jack Barton was a bit annoyed about that. He said, 'I don't see how we can release you again.'

I said, 'Well, fine. Then I'll give in my notice.'

I wanted so much to do *Open All Hours* with Ronnie Barker, one of my heroes. I'd been in the series once before, in 1976, just after I'd come out of *Coronation Street*, playing Vera Hopkins in the corner shop, so it had seemed quite funny to be going straight into another corner shop in *Open All Hours*. Ronnie Barker's professionalism was a revelation. At the first 'plotting', he had to know exactly where everything was in that shop. 'Now where's the tea? Where's the sugar kept? Where's the butter?' And he had it all blocked in his mind, so he knew exactly whether to turn this way or that way. That is a real professional.

So when I was invited in again, I definitely wanted to do it, and finally Jack Barton agreed, 'Oh, all right. But you must come straight back.'

I was only doing three episodes, so I wasn't away long. The sad thing was, after I'd done my last episode, playing Mrs Blewitt, Roy Clarke – who wrote *Open All Hours* as well as *Summer Wine*, and has such a wonderful ear for words and how things can sound funny – said to me, 'I've written the next series – and you're in every episode.'

I said, 'Oh Roy! When do they start?'

He said, 'I think we'll be starting rehearsing in about a month.'

I said, 'There's just no way I can do it. I have to go back to *Crossroads*.'

I was so disappointed. It turned out to be the last

series they ever did of *Open All Hours*, because Ronnie Barker and David Jason were both getting offered so many other things, and it became impossible to get the two of them free at the same time.

I had originally gone into *Crossroads* as part of a storyline. When I first arrived, for some reason Paul Henry, who played Benny so brilliantly, wasn't at all pleased. I've never known why. I said, 'Hallo. I'm playing Miss Luke.'

And he was very offhand and really a bit frosty. I suppose he just wondered, 'Who on earth is this?'

But after two days' rehearsing, he came to me and said, 'You're lovely, aren't you?'

I said, 'I don't know. Am I?'

Paul played Benny, a backward boy, living at the farm with his uncle. His uncle was taken into hospital, so I went in as housekeeper at the farm to look after Benny. The uncle never came back, so I stayed on for the next seven years. We became very close. Doris Luke was a very strong character, with a heart of gold. Paul Henry as Benny was – and is – a joy to work with. Paul was so funny and clever, the actor, but when he was playing Benny, you could almost see him trying to think of the words, even close up to him; it looked so real, the struggle. Then he would wink and say to me, 'Only another five minutes, kid, and we're on overtime. Make it last.'

After a time, the powers that be thought the farm was getting too popular, and were asking, is this a story about a motel, or is it a story about a farm? So they decided to cut the farm out altogether, which I always thought was a shame. I can't remember the storyline, whether the uncle died and the farm was sold, or what happened to it, but Benny and Doris moved into the motel. Doris went as the vegetable cook, and they had Benny working in the garage, which I always thought was rather unlikely.

Over the years, Miss Luke was in the post office and in the general store for a time. She was a survivor. It was a lovely part to play. She had little bits of comedy, and little bits of drama. One time she got mugged at the farm, and Benny came in and found her. It was a beautiful scene. He picked her up like a child and put her in a chair. That was done because so many old people were being mugged, and they wanted them all to have a chain on the door. So that storyline was brought in especially to encourage people to think, 'If Doris is having a chain on her door, I'll have a chain on my door.' They used to do that in *Crossroads*, try to help people with the social problems of the day.

Another good thing was the way that Paul's character, Benny, brought the problems of people with learning disabilities to the fore. It did a lot to help people's understanding. 'Miss Diane', beautifully played by Sue Hanson, tried to teach Benny how to read. Sue is such a lovely actress. She kept that character of Diane fresh all the way through. You could hardly believe her relationship with Benny wasn't real, sometimes, it was so moving.

Once we nearly had Miss Luke and Benny starting up a little guest-house on their own. His father died and left Benny quite a lot of money, and we had a beautiful scene, very difficult to play without crying, where Benny inherited all this money and bought Miss Luke a house with it. She said, 'But I can't accept it, Benny.'

I sometimes think it was a pity we didn't keep the house and leave with Miss Diane to start up our own series in it!

Crossroads was definitely the happiest show I have ever worked on. We had a wonderful time. I arrived the same day as Lynette McMorrough a lovely, bubbly person, with a funny little high voice. She still comes on the phone sometimes and I know immediately who it is as soon as she squeaks, 'Hallo!' Pamela Vezey, that wonderful actress, came in as her mother. Maggie John came in as the doctor's receptionist, another lovely character actress. She had a part in *Summer Wine* once, as Foggy's girlfriend in Wales. These women are all friends for life, but life wasn't long for dear Pamela, who died of cancer in 1992.

Harold Wolfenden was stage-manager and he was excellent. He and his wife, Jess, are now two of our greatest friends. He'd done years in repertory as leading man and producer for Frank H. Fortescue, who used to put repertory productions into theatres all over the country. On *Crossroads*, Harold really kept us up to the mark. It was very hard work.

In the very beginning *Crossroads* had gone out 'live', five days a week, which was when it got the totally unfair and undeserved reputation for collapsing scenery and fluffed cues, but by the time I went in it was all being recorded. We had to do four episodes a week. We'd be given all four scripts at the end of work on Friday, and have to be ready to start work at ten o'clock on Monday morning. We would 'block' the first episode, that is learn our moves, from ten o'clock until half past eleven. If you weren't in the first episode, your call was at quarter past eleven, ready to begin at half past, and we'd block the moves for the second episode, from half past eleven until one. Then we'd have lunch. Episode three was blocked from two o'clock until half past three, and episode four from half past three until five.

They kept to that schedule very strictly. With a lot of television programmes, the producer just calls everybody in, and you have to sit there for hours, all day sometimes, for your little bit to come, but *Crossroads* was always very well organized, and you weren't called until you were needed.

It was the same on Tuesday. We used to work all day for a fixed period on each of the episodes. Then on Wednesday we did the technical run, where the technicians came in to see which sets were being used for what, and to rig all the microphones and lights. That would be followed, on the same day, by the producer's run, when Jack Barton would work with the actors on details of their performance.

On Thursday morning we were in the studios to record episode one, Thursday afternoon episode two, Friday morning episode three, and Friday afternoon episode four. We always had to finish recording at eight o'clock at night, whatever happened. There was a minimum of eighty minutes of programme recorded every week. The episodes were either twenty minutes or twenty-two minutes long, depending on the advertisements.

So it was very hard work, but it was made so enjoyable because we all worked so well together. Everybody loved being in *Crossroads* and kicked up an enormous fuss when their character was written out, because none of us ever wanted to leave. We had a greenroom and they'd call you from there just before you had to go on the set and do your next scene. They didn't call you in until the previous scene was finished. Those of us waiting in the greenroom used to run through the scenes. We'd read through the lines together, so we all knew just what we were doing when we went in to the rehearsal room. There were no prima donnas on *Crossroads*. Most of the cast were very down-to-earth. You had to be, to cope with the amount of work that had to be done. I always said if you could do *Crossroads*, you could do anything.

I made some wonderful friends. We were all working away from home. When you're doing something in London, 90 per cent of the cast will live in London, whereas we were all away from home, apart from Noel Gordon, who had a little house in Birmingham, and Paul Henry, who was a local lad. Monday and Tuesday nights we were all still learning our lines, but after the Wednesday rehearsals, we began to feel quite free. We used to go to a theatre, or out for a meal. If you weren't in the second episode you could go out again on Thursday night. On Friday night, as soon as we'd finished, by eight o'clock, pooff, we'd all be off home. Then the whole thing would start again on Monday morning.

Another one who has become a lifelong friend is Angus Lennie, a very funny actor, who used to play Shughie, the chef. We once had a storyline when Shughie has a date with a lady he's just met. Doris says to him, 'Well, you must make yourself look nice. Wear a nice shirt and tie.'

'I haven't got any nice shirts. The collars and cuffs are all worn.'

So Doris, who was always so motherly, says, 'I'll turn them for you.'

Turning the collars and cuffs – now, that's something nobody does any more, isn't it? But that's what I did in the story, turned his collar and cuffs to hide the worn bits.

At the weekend I always used to get home to a lot of fan mail. I had more fan mail from *Crossroads* than I've ever had from anything else – stacks and stacks. After this particular story, a parcel arrived, and I thought somebody had sent me a present. I opened it, and the letter said, 'You made Shughie so happy when you turned his collar and cuffs, so I wondered if you'd do mine . . .' and this man had sent me six old shirts.

I said to Jack Barton, 'Whatever should I do?'

He said, 'Oh, give them to wardrobe, let them do them, and you can just send them back with a little note.'

So some kind person in the wardrobe department did them for him. I wouldn't have known where to start. People really believed it all.

Jack Barton, the producer, was another very funny man. You never felt he was 'the big chief', he was always one of the boys. He used to join us in the canteen, and sit and chat with us. He'd started life as a 'hoofer' as we call it, a dancer, in variety, and the tales he used to tell; how he had helped to set up Woburn Abbey as an attraction; and how the Duke and the Duchess of Bedford had a little problem, because he liked to read in bed but she didn't, and she was always complaining about the light, so the Duke asked Jack to find him a miner's lamp, with a light on the front, so he could read in bed.

*   *   *

The critics did nothing but slate *Crossroads* all the time. *All the time.* No credit was ever given for our having done anything good. They just weren't fair at all. All this talk about our never doing retakes if things were wrong; it's nonsense. It was just like all television – if you forgot your lines, you did it again. If something went wrong, we did it again. When it first started, they were doing five episodes a week, and it was all live, so, of course, things were bound to go wrong sometimes, and it couldn't be helped. All that had changed long before I went in, but the critics never changed their old tune. We had excellent people, all very experienced actors: Ronnie Allen, Tony Adams, Sue Lloyd, and Noel Gordon, dear Nolly. Some of the scenes could have been shown without disgrace in something like *Play for Today* and yet all the critics can still say is, 'They kept forgetting their lines. The scenery fell over.' It just wasn't true.

They are now repeating it on UK Gold. We've been doing publicity, and we had a photo call, and the organisers said they had never had such a response – all the newspapers wanted to send photographers along. And yet, even now, what did they all write? 'The day of the bad soap is not finished.' They put that underneath our picture, and we were there thinking we were helping to sell *Crossroads*. And you wonder, 'Why, after all these years?'

Whatever anyone says, that was the happiest programme I have ever worked on, with the best of people, and the friends I made on *Crossroads* are lifelong friends.

14

Code-name: 'Legs'

Every year around Eastertime, the *Daily Star* gives Golden Star awards to people who had done brave things, and brave children, especially, are often singled out. There would be a luncheon at the Savoy in London, and they would have a celebrity sitting at each table, so that the people getting the awards and their families all had a bit of fun during the meal.

I'd been invited to one or two of these Golden Star award ceremonies in the past, so I wasn't surprised one day in March in 1984 when the producer of *Crossroads*, Jack Barton, came to me and said, 'We've had a letter from the *Daily Star* asking if you can go to the Golden Star awards lunch next Wednesday.'

I said, 'Oh yes, I've been before.'

'Would you like to go this time?'

'Well, the trouble is, it's on a Wednesday. What about your producer's run?'

'Oh, well, it won't matter for once. Actually there are quite a few children getting awards this year and, as you know, we have the storyline coming up when you're going to help look after Glenda's baby.'

The storyline was that Glenda, played by Lynette McMorrough, was going to have a test-tube baby. Lynette was married to one of the cameramen who worked on the programme, Simon Albu, and she was really pregnant, so we followed her pregnancy all the way through, and then when the baby, Emily, was born, she came into the programme as the newborn, supposedly test-tube, baby. Doris had to help look after her, and after a while the story was that poor Doris went a bit cuckoo and ran off with the baby.

Jack was saying casually, 'Actually, it would be quite good publicity for us if you did go down, because we could take your photograph with all these little children who have done brave things.'

Well, it sounded quite plausible. I wasn't suspicious. I said, 'Yes, well if you're willing to let me have next Wednesday off, it would be lovely.'

So I travelled down on the train from Birmingham on Wednesday morning, with Jill, the publicity girl from *Crossroads*. I enjoyed the lunch at the Savoy, and I was photographed with the wonderful children who had all been very brave. Then Jill, who had wandered off somewhere, came back and said, 'Thames Television have just been on the telephone and wondered if you would go over and do a little interview for *News at Ten*, with the children?'

I was very surprised and said, '*News at Ten*? I can't stay that late. I'm in the studios tomorrow.'

'No, well,' she said, 'they said they could do the interview at seven o'clock, record it with you and the children, and put it out at ten, on the news.'

'Can they do that? And will that give us enough time to get back for the train?' I asked.

'Oh yes, I've checked that, and there is a train that will get us back.'

So I said, 'Yes, well, all right. I'll do that. It'll be nice.'

She went off to telephone and came back and said, 'I've told them you'll do it, and they've been very good, and they said that as you're staying in town until seven o'clock, they'll give us a car.'

Now, I should have known. This car was to take me anywhere I wanted in London. 'My goodness!' I said. 'How wonderful!' But I should have known.

There was just me and Jill, the publicity girl, and by this time it was about half past four. She asked me where I wanted to go, and I said, 'What shops will still be open?'

'What about Harvey Nichols?'

'Yes, that would be good.'

So we went to Harvey Nichols. Then after a bit she said, 'Would you mind coming with me to Harrods next? I've never been there and I'd love to have a look round.'

I said, 'Are you sure they'll still be open? I mean, I don't mind, I'd love to.'

'Yes, I've checked. They'll still be open.'

So the car took us and let us out at the side entrance, and the chauffeur said, 'I'll wait here for you.'

I was growing extremely puzzled – but I should have known something strange was going on.

We went in, and she said, 'I'd like to look at bedding. Do you mind coming with me?'

'No. I don't mind. I don't mind what I do,' I said.

We were walking through women's wear, and I saw a camera out of the corner of my eye, and I said, 'Oh dear, there's a camera over there. They must be setting up for a mannequin parade.' And I deliberately went the other way, which I always do whenever I see a camera.

We got to the lifts and Jill said, 'It's the sixth floor' and pressed the bell. Suddenly a lift arrived behind us, on the other side, so I was running across to catch it, and she called out, 'No! No! Don't go in that lift!'

'Whyever not?'

She said, 'Well . . . um . . . um . . . it's making a funny noise.'

You know how it starts to ping when the light flashes? – ping, ping, ping, ping, ping – to make you hurry up. I said, 'It's only the light thing . . .' but by this time the doors had closed. So we stood there again, and the other lift arrived, and I went to get in . . . and the whole cast of *Crossroads* were standing in it. I couldn't believe it. I'd left them all in Birmingham that morning, getting ready for the producer's run. I just stood there, gawping at them in complete amazement.

And then, Eamonn Andrews came out from behind them all and said, 'Kathy Staff, this is your life.' I still couldn't believe it. Eamonn took me away by car, with the producer, and I said, 'Does John know?' and they said, 'Don't ask any questions.'

We drove to the Playhouse Theatre, Kingsway, which Thames used to use, and because there was an audience still waiting to go in, we had to drive round the block again. Eamonn said, 'You mustn't get out, you mustn't be seen.'

And when I did finally get out of the car they flung a coat over my head, like a prisoner, so nobody could see who it was. They put me in a dressing-room on my own, where I found a few of my own dresses from home hanging up for me to choose from, so I thought, 'Oh, so John does know.'

John had actually stayed in London the night before, but because I had been staying in Birmingham, I didn't know. All the family had stayed the night in a hotel. They'd all been in the plot for weeks, but honestly I had not a clue. That night, after the programme, I stayed with them all in the hotel, and got the train back up to Birmingham the next morning.

The Thames Television code-name for me, when they had been setting up the whole thing, had been 'Legs'. I've still got the Big Red Book, with the script and the photographs they showed, and everyone who was there, all black and white in those days. John, Katherine and Susan were there. My sister Con, and her husband Derrick, were there, but not their two girls, my nieces Alison and Helen, which was a terrible shame. And I was very disappointed that neither Jan Davies – one of my dearest friends, who I always stayed with when working in London – nor our oldest and closest friends, Sheila and Jim Burton, were on the programme. Unfortunately they're only really interested in getting theatricals on.

All the *Crossroads* cast came except for Noel Gordon, who had just left the series. And most of the *Summer Wine* cast, including Joe Gladwin, Peter Sallis, Bill Owen and Jane Freeman, who I was supposed to be meeting the next day in Birmingham for lunch. I said, 'You might have told me.'

I was surprised and delighted to be greeted by Doris Hare. I had done a very funny charity show with Doris, and Peggy Mount. We'd had all the leading men from different West End shows singing, 'Standing on the corner watching all the girls go by' and Doris, Peggy and I – done up as Nora Batty – had come on as 'the girls'.

They had even dug up old friends from my repertory days of 1949. One boy, Richard Jeffree, told the story about the problems with Sally the dog when I was Elizabeth Barrett in *The Barretts of Wimpole Street*. Mimi Gale, my dear friend, came on, and Yvonne Fisher, another leading lady with the International Players.

Gerald Harper was on, but he was working, so he was recorded. Then there was John Schlesinger, also on video, talking about my playing Mrs Oliphant in *A Kind of Loving*, his and my first ever film. (I had only had two tiny scenes in it, playing Thora's neighbour, but I'll tell you more about that later.) Roy Barraclough, my mate, came all the way over from Germany to be on.

Irina Baranova, a ballet star, was the final guest. That was funny. John must have told them about the time when he and I had gone to a cinema in Llanelli one afternoon after we first met, to see a film starring John Clements, called *Train of Events*. I suddenly remembered in the middle of the film that I had a performance at five o'clock, so we had had to whip out of the cinema before it finished. On *This Is Your Life* they showed us the end of the film – which we'd never seen. And then this Irina Baranova – who was the female star of the film, a ballet dancer – came on, all the way from Switzerland.

About two weeks later, I was working on *Crossroads*, and I noticed I had one or two little spots on my neck. I went to see the nurse and she got the doctor to have a look at me. He said it was shingles. I asked if it was contagious, and he said no, it wasn't, and I'd be all right to carry on working, but not to let anybody know, or else they might all walk out. Luckily it was mainly on my body at first, so no one could see, but by the next day, Friday, a lot more spots had appeared.

John came to collect me at the end of the day, because we were supposed to be going to see *The Dresser*, a film I had just been in, but I said, 'Oh, please, just take me home.' I felt terrible. By the time Saturday came I was completely covered in spots, all up my neck, behind my ear, and all down one side of my face.

I was doing a programme from home for Yorkshire Television, and I had had to sign a big long form for the insurance, in case I fell over a cable or whatever, and it had said on it, *When were you last examined by a Doctor?*

I had put: *1959.*

What was the result of this examination?

I had put: *A baby!*

I've never been ill, either before or since, so I can only think it was the shock of doing *This Is Your Life* that gave me shingles. Not very long after that, the two girls and I were all on Roy Barraclough's *This Is Your Life*, because Susan and Katherine always used to called him 'Daddy Number Two' when they were little. I said to Roy, 'Now do be careful. I got the shingles after mine.' But it did no good. He got the shingles as well.

15

'The Wig was a Disaster'

It turned out that I'd got shingles very badly. Over the weekend, it spread all up my face, all round my ear, all over one side of my neck. I was really quite ill. On the following Monday, I rang Jack Barton and said, 'I'm sorry. I just can't come in today.' He said, 'Well, you haven't a lot to do this week. Could you manage to come in just for the producer's run on Wednesday, and then be in the studios on Thursday and Friday?' I thought I could probably just about manage that. I did go in on the Wednesday, but Miss Luke had to wear a headscarf to cover all her spots, and they filmed me from the other side. That Monday and Tuesday were the only two days that I have ever taken off work through illness.

Cliff Michelmore was supposed to be coming to our house the following Sunday to interview me for a religious programme for BBC 1 television, called *Home on Sunday*, in which, as the title implies, you are interviewed at your own home. We had recently moved, just the year before this, in 1983, to Yorkshire, to the Great Barn, Rockley Old Hall, Worsbrough. It was five minutes off the M1, but right in the country, and that was where they were coming to film me for *Home on Sunday*.

The Great Barn was a beautiful home but it had a peculiar feature in that all the main rooms – the living-room, dining-room and kitchen – were upstairs, and the bedrooms and bathrooms were all downstairs. We had brought with us a family heirloom, an ornate upright piano, complete with candle-holders, that had belonged to my grandmother, my father's mother. She had bought it for Uncle Sam, who had the wonderful singing voice. We had warned the removal firm about the piano but they had said that it would be no problem. I had imagined that the removal men might bring a pulley or something to haul it up the stairway, but they didn't.

Katherine was with me when I watched them struggle to get this piano up the stairs. It wasn't a spiral staircase but there were lots of turns. It was up two steps, turn, up another few steps, turn. In the end, one of the men was lying on his back on the stairs, passing the piano up to the man above from the man below with his feet and his hands. They finally managed it but by that time Katherine and I were hiding behind a sofa, unable to watch, hardly daring to breathe.

When we eventually moved house again, a few years later, I was all for leaving the piano behind but Susan said she wanted it. We were all curious to see how they would manage to get it down. They simply put ramps on the stairs and slid it down in no time at all, and Susan has still got it to this day.

For the programme, *Home on Sunday*, Cliff spent a day with you and you talked about your life and faith, and chose eight pieces of your favourite religious music, which were then sung for you by a special choir. The BBC producer had organised the choir from St Anne's church, Manchester, to sing most of my hymns, although our own choir from St Mark's were going to sing as well.

I didn't think I could manage to do a whole day's filming for the interview, so I telephoned the BBC Religious Television department and said, 'I'm afraid I'm not very well. I've got shingles. Do you think we could postpone it?'

They said, 'Oh no. Cliff's booked into the hotel. It's all arranged.'

So I said, 'Oh well. All right then. But you'll have to film me from the side, because I've got spots all over one side of my face.'

They were coming at nine in the morning. I got up feeling awful. I thought, 'Oh dear . . . Well, I'd better bath and wash my hair, so at least I'll look clean, if I don't look glamorous.'

I washed and blow-dried my hair and did the best I could with my face, and when they came I sat with the camera on the opposite side to my spots, so they weren't too noticeable.

We did the interview, and I think it went quite well. We did part of it in the house, and then I walked through the garden with Cliff. Everything looked nice. I told him some of the things I've been telling you about in this book; about having signed the pledge when my father and mother were giving lantern-slide lectures on the evils of drink for the Band of Hope; about starting work at the National, and then going for the student-actress job in Aberdeenshire, touring the village halls.

I told him about my mother being a nurse in the

First World War, where the motto was 'not sympathy, treatment'; and about how she hadn't liked me as Nora Batty, working with dirty old men; and about her stroke, and the strange way she had returned to consciousness when *Songs of Praise* and I were singing 'O Jesus, I have promised'.

Then, in the middle of the interview, Cliff suddenly said, 'I believe you were connected with the Conservative Party at one time?'

I said, 'Er . . . well, yes.' I was a bit surprised, because I thought he was only going to ask me about my faith. Anyway, I told him about my grandparents and uncles and aunts all being in trade. And how I'd been secretary of the local ward branch, which used to choose its own people to stand as councillors. I had stood in the local election, but I hadn't won, because then as now, the ladies did the work, the men got the seats.

Cliff said, 'It's so surprising, because with the characters you portray, most people would think you were Labour; they'd never think you were Conservative.'

Then we talked more about religious matters – about prayer, and about how I've always felt that religion was private, but that I hoped it showed in my life, because for me it was the most wonderful thing in the world.

I told him about our 'family choir' at St Mark's, Dukinfield, where we still went, even though we were living in Yorkshire, and how, in the choir, to some people I was 'young Kath', to others I was 'Mum' and to others 'Auntie Kath'.

I told him about Uncle Clem, the butcher, getting tongue for John's and my wedding for a hundred people in 1951, when we still had ration books; about

116

how both my girls were Sunday school teachers, and about how they had sung 'Vespers' when they were very tiny, and I had nearly wept with emotion.

The St Anne's church choir sang most of the hymns, but a friend, Gwen Fleetwood, sang a solo of the Lord's Prayer for me, at my request. Gwen had been one of the George Mitchell Singers, when Roger Fleetwood was in the orchestra. They married and had a family and came to live in Ashton. I met her in 1971, when I took the non-singing role of Ma Flannagan in *Summer Song*, with Ashton Operatic, and Gwen was in the chorus. It was an amateur production, but you would never have thought so. Gwen and I have been friends ever since.

Our own 'family' choir, me included, sang our own St Mark's hymn in St Mark's church, Dukinfield. Katherine and Susan, grown-up now, of course, sang 'Vespers', and the programme ended with my favourite hymn, 'The day Thou gavest', where people all round the world never stop praising the Lord. I told Cliff I hoped that they would be singing it at my funeral.

So that was it. A few days letter I received an anonymous letter. It's the only letter I've ever had like it. It read: *'You hypocrite. How can you say you are a Christian and a Conservative? Don't you know Christ was the first Socialist?'* And at the bottom, it said: *'P.S. The wig was a disaster.'*

I shrieked with laughter. I suppose they were expecting me to look like Nora Batty, and thought I'd just stuck a wig on. I only wish they'd put their name and address, and I could have replied. I've kept that letter, and I think it's funny, but I'm very glad it's the only one I've had like that.

* * *

I've not done much specifically 'religious' broadcasting, although in 1995 I did an educational religious programme for Carlton, telling the story of Zacchaeus, called *My Friend the Tree*, and they say the programme was awarded the Christian Broadcasting Council Gold Award for it, which is nice.

I do seem to have made quite a few appearances on *Songs of Praise* over the years. The first time was when I was doing a summer season at Scarborough – *The Mating Game*, with Barbara Windsor and Jack Smethurst – and they came into my dressing-room to interview me. I went along to the parish church for the recording of the hymns, too, because when people are talking about their favourite hymns for *Songs of Praise*, if at all possible I think they should be there to join in the singing, especially if it's somebody like me, who does go regularly to church.

Roger Royle interviewed me during the filming of *Summer Wine*, for the Holmfirth *Songs of Praise*. John and I both went along later to sing the hymns there, too. I was on *Praise Be*, talking to Thora Hird, on her special eightieth birthday edition.

Then they were doing a special *Songs of Praise* about Sunday schools in 1996, and asked me if I would go on that. They came and interviewed me in my dressing-room at the BBC Television Centre, where I was appearing on *Noel's House Party*. I told them a little tale about my first day at Sunday school. I had gone home afterwards and told my mother that the teacher had asked us to come the next week with a frock, and with our name written on a piece of paper. My mother said, 'What sort of a frock?'

'I don't know. She didn't say.'

My mother didn't know if we were doing something special like the Rose Queen, or the Whit Walks, and whether or not it was a fancy frock. She saw the teacher during the week and asked her, 'What sort of a frock do you want her to bring?'

'A frock? I don't want her to bring a frock.'

'Well, that's what she said. You wanted her to bring her name on a piece of paper, and a frock.'

'No. Her name and *address*.'

I did *Highway* with Sir Harry Secombe, just after he'd got his knighthood, at the Bradford Museum of the Moving Image, where it almost looks as if the figures are alive, and they talk to you.

Then they did yet another *Songs of Praise* at Holmfirth in 1997, to mark the twenty-fifth anniversary of *Summer Wine*. Sir Harry talked to Bill, Thora and me. So I've been quite a regular. Having been on it from so many different places – Holmfirth, Scarborough and London – I said to John, 'They'll think I deliberately run around the country, just to be in *Songs of Praise*.'

16

Katherine

Both Katherine and Susan went to St Mark's Primary School, where first my Dad, then Con and I had gone. Unlike me, our girls both got their eleven plus, and went on to Harrytown High School, at Romiley, a convent school. It wasn't *because* it was a convent. We thought, because it was direct grant, it would give them a better standard of education, and they both did very well there, getting good O and A level results.

Katherine started to train to be a teacher, like her Dad. She'd always loved children and said she wanted to work with them. But when she went on the practical course, as a student-teacher, working in schools – I don't know whether she didn't enjoy it as much as she'd hoped, or what happened – she gave it up. I was very disappointed. I thought she'd make such a wonderful teacher.

She went into dentistry. I think at first it was only because she had seen the job advertised and she had the right O levels, but she's stayed with it, and now she really loves it. She watches anything on television about teeth with great interest. I would hate it, but she loves it.

The first dentist she went to work for was a Mr Payne

– and his house was called Tooth Acre. Can you imagine? She told me and I said, 'Well!' Mr Payne was a bit of a hard taskmaster, so after six months she applied to work with the Tameside and Glossop health authority dental department, and she's been there ever since, about eighteen years now.

Both our girls have been brought up to be Christians, as John and I were, and they have both grown up to find their own places in the life of the church. Like me, they began by going to Sunday school, although it was much more interesting and broader than it had been in my day. For instance, Katherine and Susan were each in turn made Rose Queen. The girl with the highest attendance at Sunday school that year is the Rose Queen, and on Saturday nights through the year the Rose Queen and her retinue visit all the different churches in the neighbouring parishes. They have a crowning ceremony, a beautiful gown, and there are at least twelve or thirteen in the retinue, all the top children from the Sunday school. The little boys dress as heralds so that the boys have a turn, even though they couldn't be Rose Queen. It was very good, because when we were travelling round with the Rose Queen and her retinue, all the parents would come along to see the children. So many of the parents didn't bother to come to church at any other time; they just used to send the children along to Sunday school.

Katherine has a beautiful alto singing voice, and sings in the St Mark's choir. She also belongs to a group who call themselves Patchwork. Katherine plays the recorder and sings and Bill Hackwell and Paul Fearnley play guitars, and Bill also plays the banjo. Katherine usually takes the lead vocals and the men do the harmonies. They're called Patchwork because they don't stick to any particular kind of music, but take the best music from all kinds – Beatles' songs, folk music, religious music, literally all sorts. It's always different, and so interesting. They make a very nice sound and spend a lot of time going round to churches and chapels, and entertaining at old people's homes.

Every year the Tameside Canals Festival is held at Portland Basin in Ashton-under-Lyne. They have big craft tents and side shows all along the canal, and the Sunday events start with a service led by our St Mark's vicar, Rev. Dennis Thomas, with Katherine and her group leading everyone in the hymn-singing. John and I always go to the festival, and of course we attend the service and then stay and listen to Patchwork, who carry on performing after the service is over. On one recent occasion it fell on my actual birthday, the day I was sixty-four. I thought it was very funny when Katherine was standing in front of me singing the Beatles' song 'When I'm sixty-four'. She didn't seem to know what the joke was, so I said to her afterwards, 'Thank you very much.'

She said, 'What for?'

'Well, what am I today?'

It hadn't struck her.

Katherine married David John Riddell at St Mark's church on 9 August 1980. He is a care assistant and works at a local nursing home in Glossop. They met at a local pub in 1976 in Mottram. At the time he was a plumber, working for Manchester Direct Works. They live near us, and we usually see them every week for a meal, as well as at St Mark's every Sunday.

After a few years, Katherine discovered they couldn't have any children. We don't know why. They went for tests, to St Mary's Hospital in Manchester, which is a top hospital for gynaecology, and the specialists there told her that there was no reason why she shouldn't conceive, but they could try IVF treatment.

You're allowed three attempts at IVF on the National Health Service. I don't understand what they do, but it involves implanting embryos into the womb. Her stomach used to be very painful afterwards. It didn't work the first time. After the second time she was quite ill. She kept saying, 'No, I'm all right', but I felt she wasn't the usual Katherine, and it didn't work. After the third time she felt really sick, and again it didn't work. She couldn't have any more tries on the National Health, so I offered to pay for her, if she wanted to go privately to a clinic, but she said, 'No. I've seen the best specialist at one of the best hospitals in the country, and I feel now that this is God's way, and it's not meant that I should have a family.'

Shortly afterwards she felt a lump in her breast. At first she thought it was still the hormone treatment that was settling down after the IVF, so it was a week or two before she decided to go and see the doctor. He said she'd have to see a specialist, but he wasn't sure when he could get her an appointment. Our vicar at St Mark's, Dennis Thomas, who has had a lifetime of suffering various illnesses himself, said he would contact his own specialist, who would see her right away. He did. She went along, and he said he didn't think it was anything to worry about, but they would remove it to be on the safe side. The specialist said that 90 per cent of people are all right, and she was only thirty-four, a young, healthy woman, so he didn't think there was going to be any problem, but he'd let her know as soon as the results came back from the laboratory.

It was 1991. I was about to go away on tour, taking over from Peggy Mount the part of Madam Arcati in *Blithe Spirit*, and I had already begun rehearsing. We opened in Stevenage, and for the second week the company were travelling up to Inverness. Katherine's husband David's family all came from Scotland, so every year she and David have spent at least two weeks up there, touring all over, so they know it very well. Katherine said, 'I'll book you in at an hotel we know in Inverness, a nice bed and breakfast place, just opposite the theatre.'

John and I set off to drive up to Inverness on the Monday and stayed one night in Pitlochry. When we arrived on the Tuesday morning, the lady at the bed and breakfast said, 'You've got a letter.' It was from Katherine, and it said, 'While you're up there, you have to see the following things' and she had listed where we had to go every day, and what we had to see. We had to go to Loch Ness one day, and somewhere else the next. She'd suggested something different for us to do or see for each day of the week we were to be there.

The play opened on the Tuesday night. When John came to collect me from the theatre he said, 'Susan's been on. They're rushing Katherine into hospital tomorrow to operate again. It is cancer.'

Our first impulse was to get on a plane and rush straight home. But I hadn't an understudy for the play, and I thought it would probably make headlines in the newspapers if I walked out and left the production. We didn't feel Katherine would want that. She wouldn't want it blazing in dramatic headlines that she'd got breast cancer and was being rushed into hospital.

After great deliberations all night – neither of us slept very much – we decided to telephone Katherine first thing in the morning, before she went in, to see how she felt. If she wanted us to be there, of course we would leave immediately. She wasn't due at the hospital until lunch-time, so I telephoned her early in the morning, and there was no reply. I knew Susan had gone straight over to be with her, so I couldn't understand why there was no one there. I kept ringing the number. I said to John, 'I don't know where she is. Where has she gone? She should be there, getting ready.'

Finally I got through, and as soon as I heard her voice I said, 'Oh, Katherine! Where have you been?'

She sounded completely calm. She said, 'It's Wednesday morning. We went to the mid-week communion service.'

I said, 'Well, would you like me to come back? You know I'll drop everything here immediately if you want me.'

'Certainly not. You can't do anything. I'm going to the best place. I have a specialist there that I have great faith in. Susan is coming in with me. You must stay there. You must do just exactly what I've told you to do in my letter, and go and see all those places on the list.'

So that's what we did. We kept to that list. We went and we did all the things she'd told us to do. I don't know how, and I can't remember anything much about any of them, but we did. We telephoned the hospital every teatime just before I went into the theatre. I didn't dare tell anybody in the company, because if somebody had started being sympathetic I don't think I could have carried on. While I was Madam Arcati I had to concentrate on that, and keep everything else to myself.

Katherine was coming home on the Sunday, so we asked at the bed and breakfast to have an early breakfast on Sunday morning, and we drove straight down, picked David up from their home, and arrived at the hospital exactly at three o'clock visiting time, all the way from Inverness.

The specialist said to us, 'She's the sort of patient we love. You just feed her, and she gets better.'

She's always loved her food, Katherine. She's slim, even though she loves her food. When we arrived at three she said, 'Oh well. I think I'll have my tea before coming out.'

I said, 'Do you mind? We're here all the way from Inverness and we're waiting.'

But she wanted her bun and her cup of tea. She had to go to the Christie Hospital for six months of chemotherapy, and then for three weeks' radiotherapy. They said she mustn't drive herself, so we used to take her to the hospital for her treatment.

It was sad, the first day we took her in for her chemotherapy treatment, because they gave her this book telling her what life would be like, and saying she wouldn't want to eat, and her hair might come out, and there were a lot of other possible side effects. She read it out to us in the car on the way home, and we were all filled with dread. Then, when we were home, at about half past six, she said, 'Er. Aren't we going to have any dinner?'

I said, 'Well, I didn't really know whether you would fancy anything. You know, it says in the book . . .'

She said, 'I'd *love* something to eat.'

So we had a proper meal and she ate it all, and she never once went off her food. It didn't affect her eating and she didn't lose any hair.

Our best friends of over forty years, who were our neighbours when we'd first married, Sheila and Jim Burton, lived very near the hospital, and we'd call in on them for coffee and home-made cake every day after she'd had her treatment. That was just a little 'biting on' until she got to lunch-time.

Then Katherine went on to radiotherapy. They suggested she could stay in for that, because she had to have it every day for so many weeks. But she said, 'I'm not staying in. I don't want to stay in.' So we took her down each day for that, too, but the treatment literally only took five minutes. They just put a mark, and she lay down and had to keep very still while the X-rays were directed on the one spot. And that was it.

It did the trick. It's over six years now. She only has to go back once a year to have a check-up, and she seems to be keeping very well. So we give thanks to the Lord; he brought her, and us, safely through.

I don't know what I would have done, if it had gone the other way. I don't think I could just have said, 'Whatever will be, will be.' I would have argued with God, not saying, 'Why has this happened to me?' but, 'Why has my daughter got to go through this?' I wanted to have the cancer rather than Katherine, would have much preferred it that way, but this wasn't how it was to be. Nothing could be worse than to lose your child, but I still feel that my faith would somehow have been strong enough to have brought me through.

I believe in faith-healing, but I believe more in the power of two or three gathered together in prayer. I believe in the laying on of hands, but I wouldn't go to a special 'healing' person. I would go to my daughter and say, 'Help me to pray', or 'Pray with me'.

17

Susan

Our daughter Susan was ordained as deacon in Derby Cathedral in 1990; and in 1994, in Rochester Cathedral in Kent, she was among the first women to be ordained priest in the Church of England. My mother and father would have been absolutely overjoyed. They were so sad when Uncle Leonard was killed, who would have been the first member of the family to be a priest, but Susan, the last person in the world they would ever have dreamed of, their youngest granddaughter, has fulfilled the family dream.

Katherine looks like John, and Susan takes more after me, but I think in character Katherine is probably more like me, and Susan is more like her Dad. They both came along to take part in the programme *Whose Baby?*, where the panel had to guess who the famous parent was. The organisers decided Susan looked too much like me, so they had only Katherine on the actual programme – but the panel still guessed she was my daughter.

Susan was always the reserved one, from when they were young. She was always quiet and shy. Katherine would be the one to be off playing with her friends, and I'd say, 'Wait and take Susan with you.' But Susan used to say, 'I don't want to go.' It could have been that, like me, she didn't want to do whatever her sister did. Emmie Finneran, the teacher and later headteacher of St Mark's Junior School, said that Susan would slide silently into the classroom, slip her shoes off, make herself comfortable, and that was it, she was set for the day. She'd never move from her desk then.

The girls went on to a convent school purely because it was direct grant, almost like a private school, with a very high standard of education. But something about the religious life there must have made an impression on Susan, because religious studies was always her favourite subject. She took it at O and A level, and then she went to Trinity and All Saints College Horsforth, a small Roman Catholic college attached to Leeds University, to read theology.

I think a lot of it came from her Christian upbringing, and also Sunday school. When Katherine and Susan were at Sunday school, they did far more interesting things than we ever did in our day. They went to services at all the different churches to learn about the different denominations – Baptists, Roman Catholics, Methodists, Orthodox – so they could get an idea of all the different traditions of worship and ways of looking at things. Once they even went to a Jewish synagogue. It gave them a much broader outlook on Christianity and religion than I ever had. I only ever went to the one church school, and to the one evangelical Anglican church.

It gave Susan an interest in religion, not just in the Church of England, or the Roman Catholic, Methodist or Baptist churches, but in the whole of Christendom. Trinity and All Saints College encourages its students to be interested in the media. At first we thought Susan might want to have a career in religious broadcasting in television, on the production side. I always thought she would be very good at that. She is still my best critic. She's far more likely to say, 'Why did you do that?' than 'Oh, you were wonderful.' Even as a little girl she used to watch television and say things like, 'It would have been better if they'd done such-and-such.' I'd often think, 'Yes. She's right. That would have been better.' I thought she would have done so well, starting out perhaps as a researcher on religious programmes.

It sometimes works against children with parents who are already in the business. She did apply for a job, but she didn't get it. She had a degree in theology, and she knew a lot about the business from me. I would have thought she would have been absolutely ideal. But it was no good. The BBC were only taking people for training if they'd had some theatre experience, which of course she couldn't get because she wasn't a member of Equity. I got her some forms and she filled them in, but no.

We had a director on *Crossroads*, Michael Hart, Tony Hart's brother, who moved from working with us to being head of religious broadcasting for Central Television. He said to me, 'Isn't your daughter interested in working in religious television?'

I said, 'Yes. She is. She'd like to be a researcher.'

'My department will want a researcher, and that's why I'm mentioning it to you. I think she'd be ideal. I'll send you the form.'

I gave her the form, she filled it in, and I'm not sure that she didn't give it to me to take back in

person, rather than risk the post. At any rate, I know
we sent it in.

About three weeks later I ran into Michael Hart
again and he said, 'Did your daughter decide not to
apply for that job?'

I said, 'No. Why? She did apply. I took the form in
myself.'

'I was never shown it. We've just taken on somebody
from radio, a presenter.'

He never even saw her application. Susan always
says, 'Well, it was God's will.' God obviously wanted
her to work elsewhere for him.

Her first job after leaving Horsforth was at the
Christian Alliance Centre at Waterloo, not far from
the Cut, just as you're going towards the Old Vic, on
the left, a lovely old building. It's a Christian hostel for
students working in London, whatever their creed. It
was opened by Dr Coggan when he was Archbishop
of Canterbury. Susan was receptionist and secretary
there for three years.

Through Susan joining the Arts Centre Group – an
organisation also based in Waterloo, which supports
Christians in the entertainment business – I got to know
Cliff Richard. I went with Susan to an ACG meeting
one night, and he was there. He was telling us about
his faith. He wasn't standing on a stage proclaiming
it. We were all of us just sitting round, talking about
our Christian beliefs and how they had affected our
lives, and he was one of us.

Cliff said to me, 'We ought to play the London
Palladium, do a pantomime together. I've always
wanted to play Buttons. You could be my Fairy
Godmother.'

We haven't done that, but I did do a big charity show with him. For the very first Red Nose day, for Comic Relief, we were both at the Shaftesbury Theatre. Cliff sang 'The young ones', of course! Ray Cooney had written a ten-minute farce for Timothy West, Roy Kinnear, Alfred Marks, Wanda Ventham and me. It had a minimal set with only one door, which was used for every entrance and exit, of which there were well over fifty in that ten minutes. This hectic performance was directed by Leslie Lawton, another great friend of mine and a wonderful director. He also directed me in *See How They Run,* and appeared with me in *Two into One* at the Shaftesbury.

After three years at the Christian Alliance Centre, Susan was unemployed for a short period before she went, in 1986, to work at the Scripture Union for two years, as assistant to the families' adviser, Joan King, who used to run weekend workshops at different churches to help bring family members of all ages into church life; organised national conferences; and evolved projects like one called Scrap Happy, involving the Footprints Theatre Company, creating a Christian pantomime with the theme 'everyone has worth'. Susan's part was generally the administrative work, but Joan King always liked her assistants to be people she could bounce ideas off.

During the time between leaving the Christian Alliance Centre and joining the Scripture Union, Susan had been wondering about what God was calling her to do, and wondered at first if it might be missionary work. She read the biography of Hudson Taylor, who had founded the China Inland Mission. It struck her that Hudson Taylor had lived his life by the principle 'trust and obey', and she felt God saying to her, 'And you know what you have to do.'

She thought that that was to tell her vicar, Richard Bewes, Rector of All Souls' Langham Place, where she sang in the choir, that she felt God was calling her to ordination.

From that moment she began to feel that she had a vocation to go into the church. I did wonder at first which denomination she had in mind, because she'd been involved with so many, but it was the Anglican church, her own original family church, that she felt the call to work in.

In 1988, Susan went to Ridley Hall in Cambridge, where she only had to do two years instead of three, because she already had a theology degree. When they finish their training, ordination students can't simply be ordained and then look round for work. They have to find a job as a curate in the church, *before* they can be ordained as a deacon. I didn't realise that, did you? I thought you'd get some kind of certificate.

Susan was offered a job as curate to the vicar of All Saints', Mickleover, Derby, a very beautiful, ancient church. The vicar, Rev. Alan Havard, was very charming, quite an elderly gentleman. He must have been really taken with her, because he offered her the job right away, but she said, 'I want time to think about it.'

When she told me, I said, 'You can't think too long.'

She said, 'Yes, but it isn't a job like working in an office. This is going to be my life. So I've got to be sure.'

She asked him if she could go and attend the services

and see what sort of ministry it was. She went to stay for a weekend, and then returned to Ridley Hall. I said to her, 'Did you give him your answer?'

'No. I'm still thinking and praying about it.'

Poor man, he must have got het up, because he actually telephoned the Principal of Ridley Hall and said, 'Can you please try to persuade Susan to agree to come?'

So she did accept, and then she was ordained at Derby Cathedral. She was very happy at All Saints', Mickleover; it was a lovely ministry, with just the two of them. Then, after three years, she felt it was time to look for a new challenge, but the Bishop of Derby told her that he was afraid they didn't have any suitable openings at the moment, so if she wanted to move, she might need to apply to other dioceses.

She saw a post advertised in the *Church Times* to join a team ministry in Kent – St David's, at Lordswood, near Chatham – and she applied. She got a letter back saying they wanted all the applicants to go down there for a weekend, to go to the services and meet the people, followed by the interviews. Unfortunately the particular weekend they had chosen was one on which she had arranged for Joan King, the Scripture Union families adviser, to come and hold a seminar in her church in Mickleover. So she wrote to the Lordswood people to say that she was very sorry, but she could not attend, because she had things organised for the whole of that weekend. They wrote back and suggested that she go down on the Monday instead, and stay overnight. By then they would have interviewed all the other applicants.

So this is what she did. She went down on the

Monday, and came back on the Tuesday. Once again, she was offered the job almost on the spot. Once again, she didn't accept immediately. She liked the vicar, Rev. Paul Longbottom, and the Methodist minister, Paul Arnold, very much. It was only a small doubt she had this time, but at Lordswood and Walderslade they had two brand new churches, neither of them anything like as beautiful as the ancient church she had grown to love at Mickleover. She asked if she could go down the following weekend and attend some of the services and, after that, she decided to accept. Then, just before she left Derby to join them, came an historic moment.

In November 1992, the General Synod of the Church of England, after much debate and heart-searching by all concerned, passed the measure that meant that from then on, for the first time in its history, women could be ordained as priests in the Church of England. Immediately the vicar of Walderslade and Lordswood telephoned Susan, who was still at Derby, and said, 'I want you to know that I will be delighted to offer you for ordination as a priest.'

It was such a wonderful ordination service at Rochester Cathedral, the second oldest and one of the loveliest cathedrals in the country. Susan and sixteen other women were ordained on 29 May 1994, on a beautiful day. The day before had been rainy and miserable, but on this one day the sun shone.

At the end, as all the newly ordained women priests were processing out from the chancel, the whole of the congregation rose to their feet and applauded. We were singing a hymn, and you could see the girls were trying to sing, but most were quite overcome by emotion.

When they got outside, who should be waiting there but women from the nearby Roman Catholic church, and from the Movement for the Ordination of Women, waiting to give them each a posy. You felt, suddenly, we were all together as one. The women had brought everyone together.

I can't describe adequately to you how marvellous it was. God lifted us all that day. It was just the most wonderful experience.

And she's been so happy. I have been a bit disappointed, I must say, in the way the Church of England has behaved since the Synod voted for the ordination of women, with still some bishops being appointed who are against women priests. I think once we've decided which way we're going, we should all get together behind that. But even our own vicar at St Mark's is adamant against women priests, and I know there are quite a few like him. I hate to see the church being torn apart like this.

In the end it will be the achievements of the ministries of women like Susan which will win the argument, I believe. She's got a very strong calling, and now, in 1997, she's just started a new job in a team ministry as vicar at Milton Keynes. There were three interviewees for the job, two men and Susan. She had just got home from the interview, walked in and thought she'd make herself a cup of coffee and sit with her feet up for a few minutes, because she'd driven all the way back to Kent, and before she'd even made the coffee the telephone rang, and they offered her the job. She said, 'Why do they do this to me? I didn't even have time to think about it.' It was a big decision to move, as she enjoyed working with her new vicar, Rev. Stephen Morris, and Methodist minister, Keith Lemar, both having succeeded the ministers who originally appointed her to Lordswood.

Susan enjoys the whole of the work. When she first went into the ministry she thought that she wouldn't like taking funerals, but now she gets great fulfilment from doing them. She says that when people are feeling desperately sad is the one time when you can get close to them, and give them hope and understanding. She puts the time in, and takes a lot of care over it. Obviously this gets through, because she's inundated with requests to do funerals, and from the start everybody wanted 'that lovely young curate who does the beautiful funerals'.

We were staying with her at Lordswood one Christmas Eve, and she gave John a box and asked him to wrap it up for her in Christmas paper. So he did, and when we went to her Christmas Day service she had the box with her. She said in her address, 'Now we all know that Christmas is the time when God sent Jesus to live with us. Jesus was God's gift to the world.'

Then she got her parcel, and she told the congregation that inside the parcel was God's gift to his church today. She handed it to someone at the front, and they opened it and looked in. Nobody knew what was inside that box until it was passed to you and you looked inside. As we each looked in, we saw our own faces reflected back in a little mirror she'd put inside. *We* were God's gift to his church.

I just see her as my daughter. We miss her, always living away from home, but she obviously has a genuine calling and this impresses itself on people.

I sometimes think it must be a lonely life for her, because so far she hasn't found the right person who she would want to spend her life with, so she isn't married. She says she's never lonely, she's far too busy. But after three services on a Sunday, most vicars go home to a wife who has prepared a meal for them. Susan has to go home and get her own meal. But Christ didn't have an easy life, did he? She's had two serious relationships, and could quite easily still meet someone, but I think she's more interested in her work than anything else at the moment.

We're very proud of both our daughters. They're both good girls. I won't say I'm a fatalist, but I believe deeply that God organises everything, and whatever is done is God's work, God's pattern. Of course I would have loved to have been a grandmother – it would have been wonderful – but I know that God is working his purpose out. He wanted Susan to be a priest. Her calling is very strong. So who am I to say, 'That's wrong', or 'Excuse me, but I would like to be a grandmother. Do you mind?'

18

Mrs M, Alan Bennett
and Other Agents

I've been fortunate in having begun my career with two agents who both became very dear friends, and three rather unlikely extra agents. My first real agent was Mrs M, who got me Nora Batty, Doris Luke, and all my early television work, who was like a mother to me and to so many of us who were launching ourselves into the wonderful world of television in the early sixties. Later on I joined a young man called Richard Grenville at London Management, who helped me find work in the theatre as well as television, who also became a very dear friend.

At the same time I've had three 'unofficial' agents. I suppose the best one of all for getting me work has been Nora Batty herself, especially in pantomime. But Terry Wogan once helped me land a part, and so did somebody who I've never actually met – Alan Bennett.

Mrs M really was like a mother. You could go to her about anything, and we all confided in her. I never saw her without her hat. I can see her now, sitting in her office in Spring Gardens, Manchester, wearing a smallish hat, very smart, and earrings. It was a very sad day for me and many others, when she died.

Former ballet dancer, actress, impresario, agent, Mrs E V M. Mullings has died at 85 in Withington Hospital, Manchester. Christened Eleanor Nora Maud, she was known by everyone as Mrs M, which was the name she preferred.

At Covent Garden she danced under the name of Nora Maud, and married Frank Mullings, the star tenor, who she met there.

In 1917, Mrs M, who lived in Chorltonville, Manchester, joined the Beachamp Ballet, and went on to become an impresario, presenting concerts and plays at Manchester Free Trade Hall and the Library Theatre. The mother of Peter Mullings, the Granada TV Producer who directs *University Challenge*, and *What the Papers Say*, she opened her own theatrical agency when ITV was born. (*Manchester Evening News*)

Reading that obituary again has reminded me that even the elegant Mrs M once called herself Nora. You wouldn't think anyone who was dancing would call themselves Nora, would you?

I was on Terry Wogan's television chat show one day in 1989, and he said, 'Kathy, with all the things you've done, is there still something new you'd like to do?'

I said, 'Yes. I'd like to play Lady Bracknell in *The Importance of Being Earnest.*'

He said, 'Go on . . . Say "the line" . . . go on.'

So I boomed out, 'A *hand*-bag?'

Next day, Birmingham Rep telephoned my proper agent, Richard: 'Will she come and do it for us?' So I did. Thank you, Terry.

The story about Alan Bennett is a bit silly, but I'll tell you any way. In 1994 my agent Richard said he'd been asked to send me along for the part of the cook, in a film called *Mary Reilly*, with Julia Roberts and John Malkovich. When I arrived for the interview, Stephen Frears, the director, said, 'Alan Bennett told me to call you in.'

I said, 'Oh no! Not again.'

He said, 'Why do you say that?'

I said, 'I've never met him, but this is twice now that someone's said he's been talking about me.'

It had first happened when Syd Lotterby was directing *Summer Wine*. Apparently Alan Bennett had called in at his office one day and asked, 'I want the name and address of the wonderful actress playing Nora Batty.'

So Syd said to me, 'I think Alan Bennett's got something in mind for you.'

I thought, 'How marvellous.'

A few months later Syd said, 'Well? What are you doing for Alan Bennett?'

I said, 'Nothing. He's never been in touch.'

'What? He must have been. He came into my office especially . . . Are you keeping it dark?'

'No, honestly. I've never heard from him.'

And I hadn't, until, all these years later, when this film part came along.

Mrs M was quite old, in her eighties, when she died. A little while before, I had been saying that I wanted to do more work in the theatre, but Mrs M's contacts were almost entirely in television. She had got me my ten parts in *Coronation Street*. She got me *Castle Haven*,

Summer Wine and *Crossroads*. Everything in my career was established by her, and when she came near to retiring we both agreed, very amicably, that it was time for me to move on.

After a false start, I eventually found a wonderful agent in Richard Grenville of London Management in 1986, and he looked after me brilliantly, and helped me find work in the theatre as well as on television for the next ten years. He was only the same age as my daughter Katherine, and he was like a son to me. I loved him.

Richard had to go into hospital in 1987. He had begun to work from home rather than the office quite a bit, and he went on working from hospital, so I didn't realise how very ill he had been until after he was better. I had sent him flowers, but I hadn't been very worried about him. Then he had sent me a letter saying, 'I'm back in the driving seat. They're very pleased with me, because now I've learned to talk again, and I can walk and feed myself.'

Until that moment I'd just visualised him sitting up in bed with a big bandage round his head. He'd had a tumour on the brain. I saw him for the first time after he was out of hospital when he came along to see me at the BBC later in 1987, on the set of *No Frills*.

No Frills was a comedy series that went out in 1988. Mandy Fletcher produced and directed it. I played a northern grandma, Molly Bickerstaff. Belinda Sinclair played my daughter, and Catherine Schlesinger, John Schlesinger's niece, played my granddaughter. The first episode included me, recently widowed, travelling south on the train to go and stay with my daughter and granddaughter, and complaining vehemently about the plastic cups on the train, 'We used to always have a nice china cup and saucer when I used to travel down.'

Molly Bickerstaff took on everybody. She sat with two lads on the train, who were cheeking everybody, and one of them ended up holding her wool and the other winding it into a ball for her, such was her force of personality. And, needless to say, she got her cup of tea in a china cup and saucer. We filmed it all on the actual train, travelling from London up to Manchester, then staying on the train, and finishing it on the way back to London.

Janey Preger wrote it, and I thought it was very funny. She wrote a second series, and the BBC had bought the scripts because Gareth Gwenlan, who was head of comedy, thought the series was excellent. Then for some unknown reason – I don't know why to this day – Gareth Gwenlan was moved sideways and Robin Nash took over as head of comedy. He didn't want *No Frills*. I said, 'I was promised that I would be doing *No Frills*.'

'Oh no. No. But you'll still be doing *Summer Wine*.'

I was very disappointed, because *No Frills* would have been a wonderful opportunity for me. But there you go.

Richard arrived on the set of *No Frills* that day in 1987 walking with a stick, and with a patch over one eye. It came as a great shock. He was only thirty-one or -two years old. Later he had to have another operation, but then he gradually got much better. He managed to drive again, and went back to working in the office full time. He found me lots of theatre work, as I'd wanted, including parts in two West End productions.

But then, after four and a half years of getting better and better and only going back for checks, they said they were sorry, but the tumour had started to grow again. However, they said they could give him tablets to take at home so that he need not keep going into hospital.

Those tablets seemed to be wonderful. He drove down to Bournemouth in January 1996 to see me in *Cinderella*. He also had another client, Brian Cant, in the Poole pantomime, so he saw him in the matinee and then he came back to see our show in the evening. We all had a drink together in the bar. He was on top form. There was no stick or glasses or black eye-patch. He'd driven himself down and was staying in a big hotel, and we spent a very jolly evening.

He said, 'They're going to change my tablets. They say I'm a "guinea-pig" and nobody's had this treatment as long as I have, and they don't know what effect it's having on me. Something about it might be killing my red blood cells. But I don't want to change. As long as I can keep going as well as I am, I don't care about any side effects.'

But shortly after that they must have made him change. He started having to take more and more time off work. He came in to work when he could, but sometimes it was very difficult to understand what he was saying, because whatever the new treatment was, it was affecting his speech. Then he got to the stage when he was away more than he was there. I went along to the office later in 1996 to take him some chocolates for his birthday and he wasn't in, but they said, 'When he's well, he does come in. We never know when it will be.'

They didn't seem too concerned, however, so once again I didn't realise quite how serious his illness had become. Then Jean Diamond, a very experienced senior agent with London Management, asked me if I'd like her to look after me until Richard was better. *Summer Wine* was being renegotiated at that time, and I needed somebody to act for me, so I was very grateful. Then one day she telephoned and said, 'Richard's going into a hospice.'

'Is he that bad then?'

'We-ell. We thought everybody ought to know.'

Within two weeks he was dead. It was only six months since I'd seen him looking so well in Bournemouth. I think it was the hospital's fault. They changed his treatment when he didn't want it changed. Shouldn't we have the right to refuse different treatment if one kind is suiting us?

Jean Diamond has continued to look after me, so I'm in very capable, experienced hands. But Richard was like a son. He was only forty when he died in 1996. He was a wonderful agent, always there to talk to if you telephoned, a good and sincere man. I miss him.

19

It's a Farce

I've always felt the need from time to time to get back to working in the theatre, the grass-roots of all acting, and certainly my own roots. Some people say that stage acting is very different from television acting. It's not. It's exactly the same performance. You usually have to move about more on the stage, to make use of the space, and you do have to project more, to get across the footlights, whereas on television the cameras and the microphones do most of that part of the job for you, but the feeling and the performance are the same.

I have only ever played one straight dramatic role on television. (I mean, apart from dragging the woman along to be hanged in *Mr Rose!*) In 1973 I was in *Within These Walls*. It was at the time when London Weekend was doing *Billy Liar* as a television series, and I played one of his aunties. Mollie Sugden played his other auntie, my friend Pamela Vezey from *Crossroads* played his mother, and George A. Cooper played his father. Young Jeff Rawle was Billy Liar. It was so enjoyable.

We'd just come out of rehearsal one evening and were all going home. I was walking along to the tube, when the assistant stage-manager came running after me.

'Kathy!' she said, 'There's an urgent phone call for you.' I ran back into the rehearsal room, and it was Tony Wharmby, who had often directed *Castle Haven*. He offered me a part in an episode of *Within These Walls*, a drama series starring Googie Withers.

My character was in prison because she'd given away all her money to her feckless family, and then, when they wanted more, she'd bought a sewing-machine and other things on the 'never-never', and sold them, for money to give to her children. In prison she had gone into herself, and they couldn't get her to speak. It was a lovely part to play, she was such a sad lady. So often I'm typecast as these comic, down-to-earth northern ladies, and I always love an opportunity to show I can be quite different.

I've told you how I came to play Lady Bracknell in *The Importance of Being Earnest* at Birmingham Rep. When I mentioned it to Jane Freeman, from *Summer Wine*, she immediately said, 'Oh, I wonder if I could play Miss Prism.' And she did. We've become a real pair, working together in the theatre as well as on television. Jane is a very good friend, and we get on as well 'off' as we do 'on'.

In 1992, Alan Bell, the director of *Summer Wine*, came up to see us when we were both in *Sailor Beware* at Theatre Clwyd. He hadn't told us he was coming, and it was a sell-out, so he couldn't get a seat. When we told the management who he was, they took him into the lighting box and he watched from there.

We were secretly rather pleased that he had come along expecting to be able to just walk in, and found he couldn't get a seat. It makes such a difference when you're playing to a full house. That's why I firmly believe they should bring down all the prices of seats. If you can have a theatre absolutely packed at five pounds a seat, it's far better than having it only a quarter full at ten pounds.

Over the past ten years, with Richard as my agent, I've given the world my Mrs Malaprop, my Lady Bracknell and my Madam Arcati. I've done *Sailor Beware* at Theatre Clwyd and on tour. At the theatre of all my young hopes and dreams, Oldham Rep, I've done *The Corn is Green*, *Friends and Neighbours* and *Hanky Park*. At Birmingham Rep, as well as *The Importance of Being Earnest*, I was in *Flarepath* the following year. I've been in two West End plays: Ray Cooney's *Two into One* at the Shaftesbury and J. B. Priestley's *When We Are Married* at the Whitehall Theatre. This last production was awarded the BAFTA for Best Comedy, and Bill Frazer won the Best Comedy Actor award that year.

I especially love doing farce. In 1993, I did *Two into One* again, at the Churchill Theatre, Bromley, followed by a tour. Prior to that, in 1987, I toured with Philip King's other wonderful farce, *See How They Run*, also starting at the Churchill. I played Miss Skillen, the lady who gets tipsy on sherry at the vicarage. She says things like, 'I always put the flowers on the altar, and the vicar's wife has been in and moved them.' You see women like her in every church.

Later on in that tour, while I was playing Miss Skillen at Croydon, a new friend, Billy Connolly, was also at Croydon, doing his stand-up comedy in the big concert hall. Every evening, as our show came to an end, his began. We had first met in 1985, when we were both guests on *This is Your Life*. The subject was the English actress, Joyce Carey. Do you remember her playing the rather superior woman who worked behind the counter of the station buffet, who was always talking to Stanley Holloway, in the film *Brief Encounter*? I didn't know her personally, but they wanted a representative from the West End, where I was at the time. Billy was there because he had done a little cameo part in a film with her. All the other guests seemed to be rather grand and famous Shakespearean '*actors*'. I didn't know any of them. Billy took one look round, saw me, came straight over and said, 'Allo! Whoo are yhew?' We got on like a house on fire from that moment.

But at Croydon he said to me, 'Don't come to see my show, will you?'

I could see he was serious, so although I was a bit surprised I said, 'All right. I won't come to see it.'

'No,' he said gravely, 'You don't come.'

Well, now we've all seen his act on the television, so I know why he didn't want me to go. I didn't go, but the men in the cast went to see him, and they said his language was absolutely terrible.

In real life he doesn't ever use bad language. I like him. I like him very much. I find him hysterically funny. But I don't like to hear anyone using bad language, so I like him on television only when he's going round Scotland, or Australia, talking about what he sees, not the stand-up routines in between. He's so good at the travelogue part. He brings out so many things you've probably never thought of before. I've been to Australia, but he discovered many more places, saw many more fantastic things, and made such good entertainment out of them. He's very clever, but I think he finds it easy. He has such an easy personality, and sees the funny side of things.

There are still things I'd like to do both on stage and on television. I'd like to do one of Alan Bennett's characters. It's so natural, the way he writes. It's just how people do speak. There aren't a lot of classic roles that I think, 'I would so like to play that.' There's the Nurse, in *Romeo and Juliet*, and Mistress Quickly, probably. They both seem to keep bobbing up, and I suppose I ought to have a go at those. But something contemporary would probably suit me better now, something new, written for today.

One thing I enjoy doing very much, and always have a lot of fun with, is being Dame Nora in the annual Christmas pantomime . . .

20

'Dame' Nora

Nora Batty, and not any of my other agents, has got me the most offers to be in pantomime, of that I'm certain. I'm nearly always Dame Nora, in some form or another, but I once played the Empress of China in *Aladdin*, and twice I've been the Fairy Godmother and the Queen in *Cinderella*.

One of the most hard-working men of theatre in the seventies and eighties was Dick Condon, the manager of the Theatre Royal, Norwich, and the first big pantomime I ever did was for him, in 1982, when he asked me to be in *Mother Goose*. I'd never been in a professional pantomime before, so I said to Mrs M 'Find out what part they want me to play, and who they are having in the lead, because I hope it's someone really good who I can learn from.'

She came back to me and said, 'He says you are playing Mother Goose.'

I said, 'I'm what?'

She said, 'You're playing Mother Goose. So there *is* someone really good in the lead.'

I said, 'Oh dear me.'

Dick Condon telephoned and said, 'Would you come down early – for the press?'

I said, 'To Norwich?'

He said, 'Yes. I'll pay your fare. Would you fly?'

I said, '*Fly* down?'

'Yes. I'm going to have a press photo call at the airport. Would you step off the aeroplane dressed as Nora Batty, please? I want them all to use the headline "Mother Goose is Flying In". You see?'

That was typical of Dick Condon. Can you imagine the publicity we got from that?

Susan took me to Leeds airport. It was mainly businessmen from Scotland on the plane, from Aberdeen and Edinburgh. I'd got on dressed quite normally, but when we were about ten minutes from Norwich, I started putting rollers in my hair. Then I put the wrinkled stockings on, then I took off my coat and put pads on, with Nora's working overall over the top.

I thought I'd better wait until all the men had got off, because I knew there were going to be cameras, so I sat in my seat in my rollers and patterned overall while they all went past – and not one of them so much as flickered an eye. It was as though a woman flying about with her rollers in, wearing her apron, was an everyday occurrence. I thought at least one of them might have said '*Hallo!?*' But no. Nothing.

At the airport there was the comedien Bernie Clifton, on his ostrich, to meet me, and all the press. There was a girl dressed up as a goose and someone else as a dinosaur, all waiting to greet 'Mother Goose flying in'. We got wonderful pictures and publicity. Afterwards I was telling Bernie how not one of the Scottish businessmen on the aeroplane had flickered an eye at the sight of Nora Batty in her pinny, and he said, 'They didn't even glance at us, either, when they walked past me riding an ostrich, and a goose and a dinosaur all standing waiting to meet the plane. They never turned a hair.'

Mother Goose was a lovely part for me and it was an absolutely wonderful production. The story is about a mother, Mother Goose, with a son, and they have no money. She finds a goose that lays golden eggs, but that doesn't satisfy Mother Goose, because what she really wants is to be beautiful. So the Demon King says, 'If you give me your goose, I will make you beautiful.'

She gives him the goose and he tells her to go and bathe in the waters of the well. She goes down to bathe in the well, and she does come out looking beautiful, but she's lost the goose, and her son doesn't love her any more, because she doesn't look like his mum. At the end she doesn't care, she just wants everything back to how it was. It's a lovely part for a woman to do, because while you're looking like the typical pantomime dame for most of the time, when Mother Goose comes up out of the well she can look really beautiful. At Norwich we had dancing waters for the transformation scene, and it was a spectacular presentation.

Yvonne Marsh, the sister of Jean Marsh of *Upstairs, Downstairs* fame, directed it and played the principal boy. Bernie Clifton is the best comedian in the business, in my opinion, for pantomime. His whole performance, which is very funny, is geared to the children. I've worked with people with bigger names who are not nearly as funny as he is. On this occasion Bernie was my son, Silly Billy Goose, with Bobbie Bennett as Bobby, another 'Silly Billy' part. Bobbie and Bernie often work together. Michele Summers, a beautiful singer, was the principal girl. She's been up to Scarborough several times since, singing on the Spar, and I still often see her. Freddie Stevens was the Demon King, the best one I've ever worked with.

As soon as I arrived at the theatre each day Dick Condon would get on the loudspeaker to the foyer, 'Children! Guess who's just walked in – Mother Goose herself!'

That theatre was open from nine in the morning until midnight every night. There was always something happening in the foyer. There was a coffee bar all morning, then lunch was served – a proper lunch if you wanted. In the evening you could get a meal both before and after the performance. He had Mother Goose teatowels, Nora Batty mugs. That's how a theatre should be run, as a place where people feel they can pop in, meet their friends. He should have given lessons. It was a real loss to the theatre when Dick Condon died in 1991, so young, at only fifty-one.

I've done three or four more pantomimes over the years since then with Bernie Clifton. He's always on an ostrich. He did the London Marathon for many years on his ostrich. He's got tiny ostrich costumes for children, and he does a dance with all the little ostriches in the pantomime.

He's wonderful with the children, but he can be an absolute terror. I remember one day I ran into him in the street and he said, 'Oh Kathy, I'm so glad I've seen you. Would you mind just holding this a minute while I get something to show you . . .'

And he passed me his briefcase. Of course, it wasn't fastened, and it immediately opened and a great shower of cutlery crashed down on the pavement.

He was picking it up, and saying to passers-by, 'She can't help it. Don't judge.'

I said to him, 'I must be mental to keep working with you.'

Pantomime is for children, and for most of them it will be the first time they've ever been inside a theatre. If we give them a good experience, with magic and laughter, and take them into another world, they'll remember, and come back, and want to go on coming to the theatre as they grow up. I can't abide comedians who put in filthy innuendoes to get a cheap laugh from the parents. It should be geared to the children, not to the adults, and when I'm top of the bill I insist on it.

There's another thing I'm always having a fight about, although I never win, which is that these days they always want to start the pantomime with the Demon. It all goes dark, then there's a flash and a bang, and there's the Demon. Quite often, when I've been playing the Dame, my first entrance has been to come in from the back of the auditorium with my broom, pretending to attack the men with it on the way through the audience, coming down the centre aisle. So once the pantomime starts, I go and wait in the foyer to come on. And the number of children I've seen there who've had to come out in the first few minutes of the pantomime starting, screaming because they were so terrified by the Demon. Children are used to watching a little television screen at home, so when they get in a theatre, and it's so big, and there's so much noise, and this huge stage, they're a bit overawed. Sometimes they're only three years old.

The mothers will say to me, 'Now what do I do? I've

had to leave his brother in, but I can't leave him there on his own.'

But the little one is screaming with terror. I can sometimes get a few of them back in by saying, 'Now you come in with me, because I'm going to shoo the Demon away and then we're going to have a nice sing.'

I'm always saying that what they need, to get children used to the noise and the size of the stage, is an opening chorus with children and the dancers doing a maypole dance or something. They always used to start pantomimes like that, but now they don't. The flash goes and the big scary laugh. So that is one thing that if I had my way I would change, to the village green and all the happy villagers doing a maypole dance. Once the children are used to it, then you can bring in the villain and the frightening effects. But they won't do it. I know they are wrong, but they don't take any notice of me.

For three years in a row I was in a Paul Elliott production of *Cinderella* with Bill Owen. They wrote it specially for us, with Bill as Baron Hardup and I was Prince Charming's mother, the Queen. I would go to see why this man wasn't paying his rent, and of course Baron Hardup immediately fancies the Queen like mad. So it was a Compo and Nora situation, but Bill played Baron Hardup as rather more of a swell than Compo, and I played the Queen with a grand, Edith Evans voice and a powdered wig, so we had great fun, playing the same sort of relationship but in a completely different style.

The first time we did it was with Lorraine Chase

and Matthew Kelly as Cinderella and Buttons, and the following year it was with Bonnie Langford and Paul Nicholas. Bonnie used to warm up for half an hour with all the dancers before the show every night, a really very good, professional girl.

In 1985 we did it once more, in Bournemouth. In June I had received an offer to be in the pantomime they were doing at the London Palladium that Christmas, which would have been marvellous, but my agent – not Mrs M or Richard, but a little mistake I made between the two – had committed me to Paul Elliott without consulting me, and Paul Elliott wouldn't release me. I was hopping mad, I can tell you. That was when I changed my agent to Richard and I swore never to do a Paul Elliott pantomime again. At Bournemouth the star was Rolf Harris, playing Buttons. Rolf sat in the wings one day and sketched me in my dress as the Queen, saying, 'I will have tea in my chamber,' and there's Bill saying, 'Why can't she have it in a cup, like everyone else?' He gave it to me and I had a copy made for Bill because it's just wonderful.

It was during this pantomine that my sister Connie's husband Derrick died of stomach cancer. This was a very sad time for all of us – especially me, as I was so far away.

A year or two later I was at Reading, playing the Empress of China, in *Aladdin*, and it was supposed to have been with Frankie Howerd as the Genie, with me as the Empress who fancies the Genie, chasing him round and round and him going, 'Ooh! Aah! Stop it, Missis!' He was hilarious. But a week before we opened he was taken ill, and rushed into hospital for a leg operation.

The pantomime was saved because the American actor George Takai, who played Mr Sulu in *Star Trek*, was over in England. He had never even seen a pantomime in his life, but he came in at the last minute as the Genie. We had to change the whole storyline. When I was chasing him, he was shouting, 'Beam me up, Scotty! She's here again!' It altered the pantomime completely, but all the young kids absolutely loved it. We had a song called 'Star-trekking' on the songsheet.

Another year or two later I was in *Cinderella* again, at Blackpool, but this time as a flying Fairy Godmother. Mark Curry, from *Blue Peter*, a great character, was Buttons. I had to sing, 'When you wish upon a star, makes no difference who you are' and teach a new little fairy how to fly.

When they first asked me if I would be willing to fly, I said I would do it only if they had a very strong harness and very good insurance. The hardest part was getting into the harness. I had to have several men to help get me into it, because it was no good a little girl coming along and saying she was my dresser, she'd put me into it. It was made of solid leather with metal buckles and it was very, very strong. The straps had to be pulled to cross over at the front, cross over at the back, go between my legs and up my back, and then be hauled together, so I was absolutely trussed up. Then I had to put my costume on over the top of all that – a larger version of the costume that I wore when I wasn't in the harness.

Then I would walk to the side of the stage, where I was hooked up to the wire when my cue came. I used to get very apprehensive at this point. I had quite a few lines with this little fairy, and then when

I started singing, 'When you wish upon a star, makes no difference who you are . . .' up I went.

Once I was up there, it was wonderful. You can move about as much as you like across the stage, and I used to twirl myself round. Sometimes there was a problem after twirling, if you finished up with your back to the audience. You had to somehow get yourself round again to face the front, without twirling too far. I was above the lights, and I could see everything, the whole theatre, and everybody's faces all turned up to watch me, some of them clapping and cheering. It really is a magical experience, to fly.

One Saturday, John organised a bus to take a party from St Mark's church to Blackpool to see the matinee, but there was a terrible storm. The promenade was closed. The sea was coming over the top. There were no trams. We'd booked at Harry Ramsden's Fish and Chip shop on the corner of the promenade. When the show was over, John said to the older ladies as they were leaving the theatre, 'Link arms.' They all had to hold each other up to walk there, although it was only 200 yards. I had to cling to a lamp post to stop myself being blown over and sent rolling down the road after them. John was so busy helping the others he started to fly too, until he managed to wrap himself round another lamp post. As he puts it, he managed to catch hold of a passing lamp post. It was terrifying.

In 1996, I was going to be in the musical, *Billy*, with my old friend Roy Barraclough. We were going to tour for six months followed by six months in the West End. We would have been doing six weeks in Blackpool in *Billy*, so I didn't make any plans to do a pantomime that year.

Then after doing all the publicity, the production fell through because the sponsors ran out of funds, and like everyone else involved I was very disappointed and thwarted. For one thing we'd all cancelled all sorts of other work, but we only got paid for two weeks.

I didn't immediately think, 'Well, I'd better look for a pantomime.' After fourteen years of doing a pantomime every year, I actually rather wanted a break. Then Paul Elliott got on to my agent, Richard, and asked if I would do *Cinderella* for him at the Pavilion Theatre in Bournemouth. I had always said I wouldn't work for Paul Elliott again after he had refused to release me to do the London Palladium in 1985, but Richard said to me, 'Perhaps ten years is long enough – do you think – to sulk?' So I agreed to do Bournemouth, and I'm glad I did, because I enjoyed it.

It was with Les Dennis, Duncan Preston and Ann Sidney (who used to be Miss Great Britain years ago) as the Prince. The first time I ever did *Cinderella* was in 1983 at Manchester Palace, and she was the Prince then. Amanda Holden, Les Dennis's very pretty wife, was Cinderella, and we had Ward Allen, with his puppet, Roger the Dog. Duncan Preston was Baron Hardup. It was a very happy, enjoyable pantomime to be in.

But I decided then, 'Next year I really will have a break, and spend a proper Christmas with my family.' When I'm in pantomime there's almost always a performance on Christmas Eve, and by the time we get back home we've only one day together as a family. Then I have to set off back, because there's a matinee on Boxing Day. So it is very hectic.

When I've been down south in the past, at Eastbourne or Bournemouth, John and I were able to get to

Susan's church in Kent for midnight communion there. I know it shouldn't make any difference who gives you communion, but to receive it from the hands of your own daughter at midnight on Christmas Eve is an experience I won't even attempt to describe. John and I both feel so happy and so blessed.

We would stay the night with Susan. She would have her family service at ten o'clock on Christmas morning, and the children would each bring one gift. She'd gather them all round in a circle to open them, and go round with a microphone; it was a very happy occasion. When she'd finished, at about twelve o'clock, we'd all drive up north, and Katherine had the meal ready and we would have our family Christmas dinner all together at Katherine's.

Pantomime is often the only form of theatre that children and adults with physical or learning disabilities can come to and really enjoy, really enter into. Usually the organisers will say, 'We've got so many in. Will you go and see them between the shows or in the interval?'

If I'm the Fairy Godmother, I always take the wand, and put the crown on the children, and they're just beside themselves. They don't know what to do, they're so excited. You can see from their eyes and their body movements, even if they can't speak, how happy and thrilled they are. They love the fantastic costumes and the lights. They love the spectacle and the atmosphere and the whole experience, the wonder of it. You feel you're giving so much pleasure. That makes it so worthwhile. I've probably talked myself into doing one next year after all now.

21

Crossroads at the Crossroads

In 1982, ATV became Central Television, and there was a new board of directors for the new company. Lew Grade had started *Crossroads,* and the new board treated it as though they were ashamed of it. Almost the first thing they did was to get rid of Nolly, Noel Gordon, the main star of *Crossroads.* Nolly had won countless awards over the years, for Best Actress, Personality of the Year, Most Popular Fictional Character on Television, everything. Every year she won something, and had certainly done her bit for the company. She was a highly experienced actress and producer, excellent in her field, and the part of Meg Richardson was made for her. Everybody loved her. Why they decided to get rid of her I shall never know.

The rest of us in the cast were particularly upset because of the way it was done. Her agent had telephoned the producer one day to say, 'It's time to renew Nolly's contract' and he had replied, 'We don't want her any more.' After the years of service she'd given, I would have thought the very least they could have done is to tell her in person, and explained. They could have taken her into their confidence, called her in to the office, even taken her out for a meal, and told her what they were doing.

Their plan was to change the format of *Crossroads*, turning it into a bigger hotel, losing the whole idea of it being a small family business. In the original story, Meg Richardson had started the Crossroads Motel when her husband died. She lived in a big house which she'd made into a motel, and her children helped her to run it. It was a family concern. The new men at Central decided they wanted to make it a much bigger place, with a sports centre and a swimming pool, which they believed more young people would identify with. So they just said to her agent, 'Tell her we don't want her any more.'

I sometimes used to drive myself down to the Strathallen Hotel in Birmingham on Monday morning, leave my car at the hotel, and take the bus from there into the studio each day, to save worrying about parking. So, on this particular morning, I'd just got on the bus when the conductor said, 'Mornin'. I see they've got rid of Nolly, then.'

I said, 'Pardon?'

'It's in the papers this morning – she's bin sacked.'

I said rather primly, 'You don't want to believe everything you read in the papers. It's not true at all.'

It was unthinkable. Impossible. I got off the bus. I couldn't get in to the rehearsal room for the crowds of cameramen and reporters. Then we were all told the news. We were horrified, and dreadfully upset for her. We all wanted to go on strike, but Nolly said, 'No, you don't jeopardise all your careers for me.'

She was always so pleasant and easy to work with,

and highly professional. She never did the 'I'm the star here and don't you forget it' thing. She was there when she was needed, she worked hard alongside everybody else. She was a very private person, so I don't think any of us were on very close, intimate terms with her outside work. She'd given up her family home in Ross-on-Wye and bought herself a place in Birmingham to save all the travelling. *Crossroads* was the main thing in her life.

I think the shock of it started the cancer which killed her. She was only sixty-two when she died. Why do they do these terrible things? And in such a cruel way. They have no thought for what they do. In the end, of course, they sacked everybody. Ronnie Allen, Sue Lloyd and most of the regular characters were written out. Sue Hanson's 'Miss Diane', one of the most popular characters, always beautifully and sensitively acted, was written out by being killed off with pneumonia or something. They say that Paul Henry's 'Benny' went into the garage for a spanner one afternoon, and simply never came out again.

I was in pantomime at Wimbledon at Christmas 1984, early 1985. One Sunday afternoon I arrived at the theatre for the matinee, and there were cameras and reporters outside the stage door, all waiting for me. As soon as they saw me they rushed up shouting, 'Kathy! Did you know Ronnie Allen and Sue Lloyd have been sacked?'

So I said, 'No.'

'Have you been sacked?'

'No.'

'Well what do you think is going to happen?'

'I don't know anything about it. I'm here doing a

pantomime. I didn't know they'd been sacked, I still don't know if they have been sacked, and I certainly haven't been sacked myself.'

Of course, in the papers next morning they all put that I *had* been sacked and was now doing panto.

The next thing that happened was that the new *Crossroads* producer Philip Bowman telephoned and said, 'Would you come to Birmingham and do an interview on the news, and tell everybody that I haven't sacked you?'

I agreed to go along to do this little interview, and said officially that I definitely had *not* been sacked, and that when the time was right I would be going back into *Crossroads*.

But I never did. While I was still doing the pantomime, I was offered nine months in the West End playing Lily Chatterton in the Ray Cooney farce, *Two into One*, and I decided to do that. I never went back into *Crossroads* which by that time had virtually been finished off. Jack Barton, who had been the senior producer all the years I was in it, tried to buy the rights and call it *King's Oak*, a series about the whole village, not just the motel. It was all agreed, and the papers drawn up, and then suddenly Central Television said they wouldn't sell it to him. It was all politics.

Philip Bowman, the new producer, told me once that he wanted to gear it towards young people. I said, 'The viewers you've got *are* young people, when they're in, and then there are middle-aged people who have children, and the elderly, who sit and watch it every day. If you gear it just for young people, you'll lose more than half your audience.' Susan was at college

The joys of filming – with Jane Freeman ('Ivy') in
Last of the Summer Wine, 1993.

With Joe Gladwin ('Wally') in
Last of the Summer Wine, 1986.

'Push the donkey'
with Bill Owen ('Compo') in
Last of the Summer Wine, 1987.

The latest cast for *Last of the Summer Wine*.
From left to right: Sarah Thomas ('Glenda'), Peter Sallis ('Clegg'),
Thora Hird ('Edie'), Brian Wilde ('Foggy'), Kathy Staff ('Nora'),
Bill Owen ('Compo'), Juliette Kaplan ('Pearl') and Jane Freeman ('Ivy').

Beautiful Nora Batty,
Queen of the Northern Shire;
Although your hose be tatty,
You've set my heart on fire;
Come leave your pigeons and ferrets
(but bring your Summer Wine)
Come live with me in my Tower-Block Flat
(but please! Oh please!
don't bring your hat!)
And be my Valentine

Nimrod

A valentine for Nora.

As Mrs Blewitt in *Open All Hours* with
Ronnie Barker, 1982.

As the Bombazine Woman in *The Dresser* with
Tom Courtney, 1985.

As Mrs Tickett in *Little Dorrit*, 1985.
(Photo by Lord Snowdon)

As Mrs Kent the Housekeeper in *Mary Reilly* starring Julia Roberts and John Malkovich, 1994.

As Mrs Northropp in *When We are Married* in the West End, 1986.

As Lady Bracknell in *The Importance of Being Earnest*
at Birmingham Rep, 1989.

As Edie Hornett in *Sailor Beware* at Theatre Clwyd with
Jane Freeman, 1992.

As the Flying Fairy Godmother in *Cinderella* at
Blackpool, 1990/1.

Susan and Katherine, 1991.

Susan's ordination as a priest in the Church of England at
Rochester Cathedral, 1994.

My 60th birthday party, 1988. From left to right: Jim Burton, David Riddell
(Katherine's husband), Connie, Katherine, me and Sheila Burton.

John and me on our Ruby Wedding, 1991.

at the time, and she told me that it was the single most popular programme with all the students. So I don't know what they thought they were up to. We used to regularly get up to fourteen million viewers, four times a week. I've never had fanmail like it, before or since. It was absolutely fantastic.

The last storyline I had was that my sister had arrived and we had bought a house together. She was rather a dominating character, and poor Miss Luke didn't really want to go and live with her.

It was quite funny, because they were looking for a thatched cottage for this bossy sister and Miss Luke to move into, and Jack Barton, who was still in charge then, was saying one lunch-time, 'I don't know what we're going to do. We've been looking for weeks, and we can't find a cottage that will do for the story.'

I said, 'Where do you want it?'

'Well, obviously it has to be in this area, and it has to look like a little thatched, country cottage, but it also has to be near a main road, so we can get all the vans and equipment to it. Most of the ones we've seen so far are miles out in the country.'

I said, 'Well, as it happens, I think I know one, because we nearly bought it ourselves.'

It was just south of Worcester, called Cobbler's Cottage. They went along to see it, and thought it was absolutely ideal. So we used it. And Miss Luke, as far as I know, is still living to this day in Cobbler's Cottage, south of Worcester, with her bossy sister who she rather dreads, in the very house that John and I had nearly bought to live in ourselves.

22

Teach Me to Live

Years ago our church was left a lot of money for church hymn-books by someone on the condition that we had the St Mark's hymn, 'Teach me to live', printed in the front of the hymn-book. I think the words of the hymn were written 150 years ago, by the original vicar of St Mark's; and I'm almost sure that the donor was the father of Willie Underwood, a solicitor in Dukinfield. If anything special happens to anyone at St Mark's, a wedding, a christening, a funeral, we always sing that hymn. John and I had it at our wedding. It was one of my choices when I made the programme *Home on Sunday*; and on another occasion our vicar, Rev. Dennis Thomas, and all the St Mark's choir came along to be in the audience when I was on Russell Harty's chat show, and Russell asked us all to sing it to close the show. I think the words would serve as well as any to sum up my own and my family's philosophy.

Teach me to live, for life before me lies
An unknown path to yonder Paradise;
Dangers abound and round me, Lord, I see
Are other paths that lead away from Thee.

Teach me to live; to play a manly part,
To choose companions who are wise at heart;
Falsehood to shun, to love the pure and true,
And ever climbing, keep the end in view.

Teach me to live; with sunny words of cheer,
To brighten life and dry a brother's tear;
Songs for the sad, a lift for heavy load,
A heart to win a wanderer back to God.

Teach me to live, Lord, arm me with Thy might,
And make me strong to battle for the right:
Ready to serve; content to come or go,
Or e'en to wait, if Thou wouldst have it so.

Teach me to live, for this alone I pray
That I might grow in wisdom day by day,
Then at the last, life's short probation o'er,
I'll dwell with Thee, my King, for evermore.

Ronnie Hazlehurst, who does all the music for *Summer Wine*, came up to me one day in the BBC Television Centre canteen, soon after I arrived there to do the very first series. He said, 'Are you Kathy Staff?'

'Yes.'

'Do you play Nora Batty in *Last of the Summer Wine*?'

'Yes.'

'Do you live in Dukinfield?'

'Yes.'

He said, 'They told me you did. And I said, "Nah. She can't do. Nobody comes from Dukinfield except me!"'

Well, as you know by now, I do indeed come from Dukinfield, and unlike Ronnie Hazlehurst, I've never moved very far away. I still belong to St Mark's, the church my parents and grandparents belonged to, where John, Katherine and I – and Susan in earlier years – all sing in the choir, which includes many old friends, and many descendants of the Higginbottoms and Hartleys, although there isn't a Higginbottom or Hartley left among us. And now the Staff family name will soon be gone too, because our family seem to know how to produce only girls. My sister Con has two girls. Her elder daughter, Alison, has two children, Hannah and Gareth, so she has got a boy – but he's the first boy born in the family since my cousin Leonard was born, Auntie Ada's son, and he has gone to live in New Zealand. Con's younger daughter, Helen, is married to Robin, who works for Age Concern.

When Con and I were children there used to be at least two hundred people in church on a Sunday, and they all sang really well, but you could always hear my mother, top notes soaring above. My father had a nice tenor voice, and Uncle Sam, my father's brother, had a wonderful voice. We used to sing Stainer's *Crucifixion* every year, and we used to invite a tenor from Manchester Cathedral, but Sam always sang the bass solo.

There are fewer people who regularly come to the church today, but we can still form a little four-part harmonising family choir in our row. Katherine sings alto, John takes tenor, Susan and I sing soprano, with Uncle Harry, aged eighty-three and not officially in the choir any more – but only because of failing eyesight – making a fine bass.

So many of the congregation are people I've known

all my life. Some of them have known me since I was born, and I've known all the younger ones since they were born, and their children and their children's children. Our daughter Katherine's very best friend is Kathryn Finneran, whose father Tom and his brother Charlie were identical twins, who I remember playing with when we were children. And Emmie Finneran, Kathryn's mother, was a teacher at St Mark's school, and ended up as headteacher. Their family have always belonged to the church as well. There's Benny Lecky, who was in my class at school. His family had a chip shop. He just loves to sing. Even when the organist is playing the introduction, Benny will be singing along on his own, and Frank Bowden who, with his four brothers, was in the choir from a very early age.

In *Last of the Summer Wine,* the women go to church and the men have to be dragged in. I think this represents a true picture of church life. I think generally women are more sympathetic to the Christian message: 'Love one another', and 'Do good whenever you can'. They find it easier to love Christ. I don't know whether the men feel it isn't quite macho. I don't say all men are the same – I have known some very devout men, in my own family and of all generations – but more women seem to accept Christ and his teaching, and that's why you get more women in the church.

It's a very hard message. It sometimes comes more naturally to hate one another and fight one another, but Christ says 'No'. It's not easy, if somebody does you harm, to turn the other cheek, and love them. It's very hard to love someone who has worked against you.

If you take your children to church, instead of

sending your children to church, then the whole family will grow together, with the same values. So many people send their children to Sunday school and leave them there, while they disappear, as though this is something not for grown-ups, just for children. Our children have had a firm Christian foundation to their lives, and I know it has stood them both in good stead. They have neither of them had trouble-free lives, but they've always been able to cope, because they both have an inner strength, which only faith can give you.

Religion has to be carried into every part of your life. I've turned down quite a few plays over the years for various reasons, sometimes when it includes people stripping and being on the stage naked. I can't go into a play like that. I'm not trying to lay down the law for anyone else, I just know I could not do it.

I turned down a leading part just recently, at the beginning of 1997. They were reopening Shepherd's Bush Theatre and they sent me a script. It was all about the miners' strike, and the pit closures. The part was absolutely marvellous. She was the mother of a family that had been split because, when they went down the mine shaft to picket the mine, they found that it hadn't been looked after, and one person was killed. It split the whole community, and split her family. It was an excellent play . . . but the language! I couldn't have spoken *so* much of it. Had it just been my own character swearing, perhaps I could have talked the writer and the director into letting me tone it down, but it was everybody in the play; the language was very strong throughout.

I am very sad when people use Christ's name as a swear word. I feel it's blasphemy and I can't bear it.

But unfortunately a lot of people do it, and in that play it was probably even right, if they wanted to portray authentically the people of that time in that situation, to use the language they would actually have used. But I couldn't do it. I don't expect other people to feel the same as me, but if you have Christian standards in your life, you have to carry those standards all through everything.

Whenever I get sent a script, John and I both read it. I sometimes like Susan to read it, too, when she's about, because her judgment is extremely good. And especially now she is a priest, I don't want to let her down by accepting things that haven't a good Christian standard. With this last play, with my sister living over in Barnsley in mining country, I asked her to read it too. So we always get various people saying what they think. They are part of it. Then if we all think there's something not right, I refuse it.

I just don't understand people who don't believe in God. I don't know how they live their lives, because I know I couldn't cope with mine without faith. It's the centre of my life. I could no more turn my back on it and say there is no God, than fly. It's just something impossible for me. I say my prayers every night before I go to sleep. I pray as I'm doing my work, as well. Without God's strength I couldn't do what I do. I'm a great believer that he has put me on this planet, has given me a talent, however small, and I want to use that talent, not only as Nora Batty, but to the glory of God.

23

The *Summer Wine* Caravan

We share a tiny little caravan up on the moor, Dame Thora Hird, Jane Freeman, and I, when we're filming; and there is a huge Winnebago for the three men. I do more filming than the other ladies, but even I'm not there all the time. The three men *are* there all the time, so they do deserve the 'number one' dressing-room, but it's become a bit of a social thing – everyone else is second-class compared with the three men. However, you can probably guess who has the most fun.

While we're waiting – and some days we can be waiting for a long time – we sometimes have a little game in our caravan. No money changes hands, but we all guess the time when we think we'll be called out to do our scene, and whoever wins gets an extra chocolate biscuit at coffee break. And, of course, Thora regales us with her wonderful stories.

There was a woman from a magazine who came to interview us all recently. She went into the Winnebago to see the men first, and then she came to us, and she said it had been like visiting a morgue in there. She came into our little caravan, with Thora, Jane and me, and she was with us all afternoon. She said, 'What a difference! I could write a whole book on each of you after this. You're all so happy in here.'

We *are* happy. We have a lovely time. I don't know why the three men seem so miserable sometimes. All I can say is, it wasn't always like that.

There isn't usually anywhere for the rest of the cast to sit. Sometimes they'll bring along folding deckchairs, if the weather's nice, for when we're waiting. There's a make-up caravan, and a few people can sit in there. There's another one for wardrobe, but that's pretty full of clothes and boxes. And we have location catering. When Thora and Jane aren't there, I let the girls come into our caravan.

They put our caravans near to where they're filming; not so that they're in shot, obviously, but they make a base near to where we're actually filming. We have a honey wagon, with three ladies' loos and a wash basin, so it's quite civilised. Even when we're filming in the town we stay in our caravans, so we're independent of the local community.

We didn't at one time. We didn't even have toilets, and I remember once we were filming on the top of the moor all day. After lunch Joe and I both badly needed a loo, so I drove him to some friends I'd made in Holmfirth, and we just knocked on the door and asked if we could use theirs. What else could we do?

We've had our ups and downs during the filming. In the very first series, there was a scene, hard to imagine now, of Nora riding a bicycle. Nora had been shopping on her bicycle, and put all her shopping in the basket on the front.

I hadn't ridden a bicycle since I was a child, so I borrowed a neighbour's daughter's brand new bicycle to practise on. I cycled around, getting used to it and rather enjoyed myself.

When I got to Holmfirth, the bicycle they had got for me was the old-fashioned 'sit-up-and-beg' type, a real old boneshaker. The prop boys had gone a bit berserk and filled the basket so full of things, I couldn't even push the bike, never mind ride it. But eventually they got it right.

The story was, Nora is cycling home, and Compo jumps out at her; she falls off, and then she starts throwing things at him, like cabbages and carrots, from her basket of shopping. I thought the only way to do it would be to let myself go, and really fall. So this is what I did. After the first take, Sydney Lotterby said, 'Oh yes. That was wonderful. Absolutely realistic. Now I want to film it again from the other side. Can you fall like that again, in exactly the same spot?'

So I had to fall again. In the end, I did it three times. You can see how important I was in those days! I could have easily broken an arm or my leg. Bill was quite perturbed and said to me, 'You know, you shouldn't really be doing this.' Fortunately, with my padding, I didn't hurt myself too much, but my knees and elbows were covered in bruises. Mrs M was very upset, because the following week I was due to go into *Coronation Street*, as Vera Hopkins in the corner shop. But I survived. What we do for our art!

A few series later, we were doing a Christmas episode, and in it the three men were all going away. Because it was Christmas Day, Nora had had her hair done, and the make-up people gave me one of those hairnets with little sparkly beads, to wear to show that Nora was celebrating Christmas in style. The story was that Nora is waiting for her guests, and Compo comes round with his ferrets for her to look after while he's away. We sometimes have to work with real ferrets. On one occasion Compo's ferrets got into Nora's laundry basket, which I found very alarming. But for this scene, thankfully they were in a cage, and they were the stuffed variety. As soon as she takes the cage with the ferrets from him, Compo lunges at her, knowing she can't hit him. But the buttons on his sleeves got caught up in my fancy hairnet, and we were absolutely stuck together. The director didn't realise and kept shouting, 'Break! Break from her!'

It was one of the funniest moments.

And then, there's the weather. We spend about a week filming each episode, but it's often a race against time, mainly because the climate at Holmfirth is a law unto itself. It can be beautiful at home, and Jane Freeman (who always stays with us when we're filming) and I can leave John saying he's going to get down to a good day in the garden. Just as we are driving down the last mile into Holmfirth we'll say, 'Oh my goodness, look at it.' It'll be dark clouds and pouring rain. We've had whole days, sometimes, when we couldn't do any work at all because of the rain. You have to have a bit of brightness, because it is called *Summer Wine*, after all. In the last Christmas episode, with the circus tent, we were all wading in water and mud. It was just terrible.

I think it would have been during the second series that Joe Gladwin and I were doing a scene together one day. We were called at seven o'clock in the morning for make-up and costume, taken out to the location, and put into the motorbike and sidecar. While we were travelling along on the low-loader, my first line was to have been, 'Look at the view', and Joe had to say, 'I'm looking at the view.'

Then I say, 'You're not. Look at the view.'

'I am. I am. I'm looking at the view.'

Well, we were waiting there, and you couldn't even see the field beside the road, it was so murky. We sat there, from eight in the morning, doing absolutely nothing, until lunch-time, and then Sydney Lotterby said, 'I don't think there's going to be a view, do you? You might as well go home.'

So we all went home.

We can have had the most terrible day there, and done nothing, and yet when we have arrived back at home in the evening, John is often still working out in the garden, having been out there all day, with the blackbirds singing and the sun shining. And we've only been a twenty-minute drive across the moor.

24

Ballet Shoes

I always loved dancing, but my parents couldn't afford to pay for lessons, so the only instruction I got was once a year, when people came to teach us steps for the pantomime. My dream was to be a ballet dancer when I grew up, but I soon realised that unless you started at a very early age with ballet, it's no good. You can't just pick it up later in life. But I have always loved it, and it's still my favourite form of entertainment. I'm a patron of the Northern Ballet. My sister Con can't get interested in ballet. Con loves opera, which does absolutely nothing for me.

In May 1990 I was invited to be in a programme called *Stargazers* at Yorkshire Television, with Richard Whiteley. They were asking well-known people to have a go at something they had always wanted to do. They gave five or six of us a chance to live out a dream. Bernie Clifton, I remember, went up in a hot-air balloon. Barry Cryer drove a tram in Denmark.

They contacted me and said, 'We know you are religious and like music. Would you like to go to Oberammergau, and we'll come and film your visit?'

As it happens, I'd already been to Oberammergau, so I said, 'What I have really always wanted is to dance in a ballet. I don't mean in a funny way, Nora Batty with wrinkled stockings and a tutu. I'm quite serious. I really did, as a child, want to be a ballet dancer.'

They called back and invited me to go along to the Grand Theatre in Leeds, where the Northern Ballet were dancing *The Simple Man*, the ballet about the life of the artist, Lowry, to dance in it with them. I accepted at once, and I was thinking, 'Thank goodness', because I knew that in the ballet they were all dressed in working clothes, and there wouldn't be a tutu in sight. I was serious about it, and didn't want to be made a Charlie of.

Sheila and Jim Burton have been our best friends since we lived next door to each other when we were all first married, and Sheila and I travelled into work every day on the same bus, and we all went on holiday together. We all four became, and have remained, inseparable. It was Sheila who had first got me involved with Northern Ballet, years ago, when she was their promotions secretary, trying to find patrons to help put on the ballets. We both love the ballet, and often go together. I said I couldn't afford a lot, but I'd give them something every year, so I became a patron, and then, all these years later, I was to be dancing with them.

I went to watch the matinee, and the ballet-mistress sat behind me and said, 'Now this is the scene we want you to be in.' There was a barrel-organ and children dancing round. After the matinee they took me backstage. Yorkshire Television filmed a little scene of Christopher Gable saying to me, 'We've got one person off sick, would you go on?'

And me pretending to be very surprised, saying, 'Oh! Are you sure?'

Then I had to be costumed. I wore a long black skirt and shawl, and a black wig with a big bun at the back. I wore black woolly stockings, and shoes that looked like governess's boots, but they were made of beautiful soft leather for dancing in. When I was watching the matinee I had noticed there was an old crone who appeared to just walk across the back of the stage, so I thought that was the part they would ask me to do. But no. I had to learn the dance that the children and the corps de ballet were doing. I had an hour to learn this dance. I have never been so petrified in all my life.

I don't know whether you've ever seen the ballet, *A Simple Man*, but the music is quite syncopated. It's never a straight one, two, three, four beats to a bar. The steps I had to do took only a couple of minutes to perform, but it was so hard to learn them. I practised and practised, and I thought I'd never get it right. I said to the ballet-mistress, 'You must think I'm so thick.'

She said, 'To tell you the truth, the rest of the corps de ballet, and the children, all took two hours to learn the steps that you've just learned in an hour. So you've definitely got a gift for it.'

I've still never ever been so nervous about anything. On the *Stargazers* film afterwards, you could see me really suffering at the rehearsal, trying to learn these steps.

Then, of course, I'd been learning it just on my own with the ballet-mistress, but when it came to the actual performance in the evening, I found I was put right in the middle of all the children. I thought if I went the wrong way, I could knock them all down like skittles.

Well, I did it. It had to be filmed from the side, from the wings, by Yorkshire Television, because it was all done at a real performance in front of a real audience. You couldn't see very well on the television pictures whether I'd got the steps right or not – so you'll just have to take my word for it, I did get them right. When we'd done the little dance, they had me on the side with the children, making gestures to them as though I was keeping them all in order. I didn't know it, but Christopher Gable had said to the dancers, 'Now watch Kathy's face. This is what you've got to learn – how to act as well as dance – so just watch Kathy's face to see how she does it.'

As soon as the curtain came down Christopher Gable hugged me and they gave me a huge basket full of the most beautiful flowers. It was wonderful, a dream come true.

Christopher asked me if I would dance with them again. I went to the newly renovated Alhambra Theatre, Bradford, where I'd been in the film, *The Dresser*, a few years earlier. There I danced – just for one performance on a Saturday night – in *Giselle*. I was one of the Court Ladies, wearing the most beautiful costume. They even added my name in the programme.

Of course, in the morning there had been a press call, to get publicity for the show, and the newspapers all wanted to photograph me in a tutu, or rather, Nora Batty in a tutu, with wrinkled stockings. I tried to say no, but they said, 'If you won't do it, we won't do any publicity for the show.' They'd actually brought a tutu with them. I knew the Northern Ballet needed the publicity, so I did it, but I felt pretty angry about it, because in neither show was I in a tutu at all.

Then Christopher Gable asked me to dance the Nurse in *Romeo and Juliet*. I went to see it, and the girl who danced the Nurse, Hayley Tognetti, was wonderful. She did a whole comedy number on points. I said, 'There's no way, at my age, that I could do that.'

He said, 'No. But you could get the comedy in other ways. We'd choreograph it especially for you.'

I was tempted, but in the end I thought, 'No. I don't want to take a dancer's job, even for one night. I've enough work.'

To go as an extra in the corps de ballet was one thing, if it got them some publicity, but take a girl's solo part – I didn't think it would be right. So I didn't do it. But I'm happy. I've had my childhood dream come true.

25

Hollywood – Here I Don't Come

I haven't been in many films, but I've enjoyed the ones I've done. The first was in 1961, *A Kind of Loving*, with a new director, making his first film, John Schlesinger. It is where I first met my long time heroine, Thora Hird, when I was playing her next-door neighbour. I had just two little scenes: one when Alan Bates comes back and can't get into the house and I tell him his wife has fallen down the stairs, and another where I am buying cakes and things for the children's tea from the Co-op van.

I had been asked to bring Katherine and Susan along to be 'extras', to act as my children playing in the garden. Katherine was four then, and Susan was two. But then they decided that the garden was too small for both of them, so Susan sat in the house being looked after by Thora, who was wonderful with both the girls, while Katherine rode her bike round and round the garden. When the film was shown on television years later, Susan always said, 'I'm there, in the house, behind the curtains.' I often say to Thora now, 'I think you must have had an influence on Susan when you looked after her that day, because now she's a priest.' Katherine was at grammar school when it was first shown on television. In the film she's aged four, remember, riding round on a bicycle, but she came home from school most indignant. She said, 'All the girls in class recognised you, but nobody recognised me!'

For those two scenes I had two days' filming on location, and a day at Pinewood Studios to 'post-synch' the sound. Films are much slower work than television. You do one shot, say one line, then they ask everyone to clear the set while they build another wall to shoot the other half of the kitchen or whatever. And you'll be waiting for anything up to an hour, before you say your next bit. They set up and light the shots with stand-ins. While you're waiting you're thinking, 'Heavens, we could have done half an episode instead of half a sentence this morning, if this had been for television.'

I didn't do another film for twenty years. Then in 1982 I was in *Separate Tables*, a television film, directed once again by John Schlesinger. I played Mabel, the waitress at the boarding-house. The stars were Alan Bates and Julie Christie, who are both very attractive actors and very lovable people. Julie Christie is always so fresh-looking as well as beautiful, but she used to arrive each day wearing a bomber jacket. Alan Bates said to me, 'I'm taking her out to dinner tonight. She's coming to my hotel. I do hope she doesn't turn up in that old bomber jacket.'

Julie was in Harold Pinter's *Old Times* at Theatre Clwyd in 1996, and John and I tried to get seats, but it was booked up. I said who I was, and they said, 'Just come along. We'll push you in somewhere.'

So we went along and they did manage to find us two seats, so I left a little note at the stage door for Julie, asking if we could say hallo in the bar afterwards.

I didn't want to go barging round to her dressing-room, because it was a long time – fourteen years – since I'd seen her, and I didn't really know whether she'd remember me or not, being the big star she is. But I thought, 'Well, if she wants to come to the bar for a chat, she can.'

So we went to the bar, and the rest of the cast were all saying, 'Oh no, she won't come. She never comes.'

And suddenly she appeared. She was looking all round, and then she saw me and she shrieked, 'Kathy!' and came running over and hugged me. It did my ego a lot of good. She had a drink, and we chatted, and she was so friendly and lovely. After she'd gone everyone said, 'We didn't realise you knew her *that* well!'

I said, 'I didn't know myself.'

In 1983 I was in *The Dresser*. In the script I was called 'the Bombazine Woman'. Albert Finney plays the Famous Actor, and there is a scene where he goes berserk in the marketplace. I'm a woman who has always been a fan of his, who tries to calm him down. I enjoyed that. Tom Courtenay's character, the Dresser, arrives and I say to him, 'Look after him. Get him home.'

And then I have another short scene with Tom Courtenay, in the theatre bar in the interval, my character having come to watch the play. It was all done on location. The scenes in the theatre were filmed while they were doing up the Bradford Alhambra, one of the first theatres in the country to be modernised backstage and have dressing-rooms with en suite 'facilities'. Very nice too. A few years later I was to dance with the Northern Ballet in the renovated Bradford Alhambra.

In 1984 I had a nice little scene in *Camille,* which was filmed in Paris, but it wasn't in French. There were lots of stars – Denholm Elliott, Sir John Gielgud, and Camille was played by Greta Scacchi. I was the lady selling flowers in Paris who gives her the camellia. I enjoyed that, too.

Then in 1985 I was Mrs Tickett, the housekeeper, in *Little Dorrit.* It was two separate films really. Ours was done, and then they filmed it all again from Little Dorrit's point of view. To my great regret I didn't get to work with my idol, Sir Alec Guinness, as I was only in the first part.

My scenes in *Little Dorrit* were with Derek Jacobi, who is another terrific actor. He went to get his OBE on the day we were filming, and when he came back he had brought it with him, and for the press they photographed him with me, looking at his OBE.

The stills photographer on the film set was – Lord Snowdon. He was so quick and clever. He said to me, 'What character are you?'

I told him I was Mrs Tickett, the housekeeper. He immediately called out, 'Can we have a bunch of keys here, please.'

In a trice he had a bunch of keys hanging down from my belt. When I was in position he looked at me, and said, 'Oh dear. I think that fingernail is a bit too long, don't you? For a housekeeper . . . ? Can we have some scissors, please.'

He then actually cut the nail himself.

It was to be nearly another ten years before I was in another film. In 1994 I had a good part with lots of scenes, as the cook in the film of the R. L. Stevenson story of Dr Jekyll and Mr Hyde, *Mary Reilly*, starring Julia Roberts and John Malkovich. George Cole was the butler. Glenn Close was the madam at the brothel. Michael Gambon was in it. A first-class cast. I haven't done many films, but this time I had high hopes. I had quite a big part and I thought, 'This is it. A real opportunity.' But it wasn't to be.

Julia Roberts was so good to work with. She insisted, when they were doing my close-ups, on standing there and giving her line, so I also had the correct eye line. That's very rare, for a big star to be prepared to stand in to give an eye line to an actor with a much smaller part. One night she'd actually gone off and changed, and when she found out I was still working, she came back in and gave me the lines.

It really should have been a box-office success, particularly over here, where everyone loves a good costume drama, and it's a wonderful, classic story. I don't understand why it flopped so badly. The American critics didn't like it because Julia Roberts didn't look glamorous. She deliberately wore no make-up. They said, 'Can you imagine Pretty Woman looking like this?' In England, the critics just kept going on about her accent. Admittedly she's not Irish, but she gets this lovely soft lilt. Honestly, there isn't much difference between an American and a soft Irish accent. It didn't worry me at all. There was nothing wrong with it. Anyway, nobody asked Kevin Costner where his Nottingham accent was for *Robin Hood*, did they? John Wayne – it didn't matter what part he was playing, whether he was in a period film or being a cowboy, he still sounded like John Wayne. Humphrey Bogart was another one; they were all just the same. So why should they pull her apart because she tried to do something different? I thought she was really good.

It all seems to me to have been so small-minded and ridiculous, but as a result, it's never been properly released over here, and it seems to have sunk without trace, and after all that money and hard work . . . Even Barry Norman said, 'It was much better than I expected. But . . .' and then he went on about her accent, and showed people like Dick Van Dyke and all their terrible accents. And that's all he talked about. He did say, 'George Cole and *Katy* Staff were good.' He didn't even get my name right.

It was certainly a big disappointment for me. They used to watch the rushes every lunch-time and say to me, 'Oh, your scenes! They're so good. Everybody's asking who you are.' I suppose it just wasn't meant to be, that's all. It's no good getting disappointed.

I don't think I'd really want to go to America anyway. When I had originally got the part Alan Bell said, 'They'll whisk you off to Hollywood to be in all the films now.'

I said, 'I don't want to be whisked off to Hollywood, thank you very much.'

26

Joe Gladwin

In March 1987, I was meant to be appearing at a charity show for Age Concern, in Kendal. We were driving up from London when the snow started, and by the time we got to Birmingham it was getting very thick, and the outer lane of the motorway was blocked. We decided we couldn't really go much further, so we stopped and telephoned the organisers and apologised, but said we weren't going to make it. I think it's the only time I've ever had to let a charity down, and I felt very bad about it, but we felt we couldn't safely drive any further. We came off the motorway at Manchester, very near to where Joe Gladwin lived.

Joe, who played my husband in *Summer Wine*, Wally Batty, was very ill. I telephoned and asked Lil, his wife, if we could come and see them as we were very near, and I heard her saying to him, 'It's Kathy. Can she come and see you?'

I heard him say, 'Ah. That would be lovely.'

We went, and I was so shocked and upset, because he was like a skeleton. He'd gone down to six stone. He couldn't bear anybody even to touch him because his body was so painful. He said sadly, 'I won't be able to do the next series, Kathy.'

I said, 'Oh, of course you will. You've got the summer

ahead of you. You'll build up your strength then, and you'll be fine.' But we both knew he wouldn't.

He seemed very tired. We offered to help to get him upstairs to his bed, but Lil said they knew how to do it between them, so we left. He became unconscious in the middle of that night. She got him to hospital, but he never regained consciousness, and he died soon after that. We must have been the last people he saw.

Joe had always been wonderful to work with. I'd worked with him first when we were both with Harry Worth on *Here's Harry*. And after that we were in *Nearest and Dearest*, with Hylda Baker and Jimmy Jewell. I don't know whether you remember, but Joe was the foreman in the pickle factory, and he used to have very thick glasses. I was 'Beetroot Bertha', and two other girls were called 'Onion Annie' and 'Vinegar Vera'. They had decided to write the three of us in to *Nearest and Dearest*, to help Hylda with her words, to ease the burden for her, really. But Hylda didn't approve of having us there, so we were only in the one series.

And then, of course, Joe came into *Last of the Summer Wine* as Wally. He was marvellous. When the scene meant that I had to pull him inside the house I just used to barely touch him and he'd jump in, hurling himself through the door as though I was really yanking him. I used to say, 'Joe! You'll hurt yourself!' but he'd say, 'I'm all right.'

Right up to the last he used to tap-dance and sing for us. He'd started on the piers at Blackpool as a tap-dancer, and he had been a 'feed' for Dave Morris, a comedian. Right up until the year he died, he'd be tap-dancing on the set for us, when there was a break in filming.

Joe was eighty-two when he died, the most lovable man, a faithful friend, and a great Christian soul. I was so glad that I had been given the chance to say goodbye to him. Once again God seemed to have worked things out without my planning it, so I could be in the right place at the right time.

Joe was Roman Catholic, and had been awarded a papal medal for all the work he did for the church. He was a Knight of St Gregory. Syd Lotterby was producing *Summer Wine* at the time, and he telephoned me and said, 'Kathy, did you know, Joe's been made a Saint?'

I said, 'Syd! Saints are dead.'

'Well, it's something like that.'

Joe wasn't a Saint, but he was a saint. He did so much for his church. Right up until the end he used to go round and collect all the old ladies from his local church and take them to Mass, and then he'd go home and pick up Lil, his wife, and they'd go to the second Mass together. They did that all their married life.

One of the familiar scenes from *Summer Wine* would be Joe sitting on the steps outside the house, and Compo and the others coming up to him:

Compo:	What are you doing, Wally?
Wally:	I'm gi'ing 'er a 'ard time.
Foggy:	Don't you think you might be overdoing it?
Wally:	I don't care. I stand so much, then I get me rag out. Then I cum out 'ere and sulk. She 'ates it when I come out 'ere and sulk.

Then out would come Nora, arms akimbo:

Nora: Here, you! Inside.
Wally: I'll come inside when I'm good an' ready . . .

One look from Nora and:

Wally: . . . As it 'appens, I'm ready now.

And in he'd scuttle, like a frightened rabbit. I really miss him.

27

Funny Ladies, Funny Men

Comic timing has to be instinctive. You can't teach it. If you miss the beat, you lose it. The great comedians and comediennes are funny without it seeming to be any effort at all. Being funny just seems to come naturally. I've admired so many of them all through my life, and they have all, in one way or another, influenced and inspired my work, so I thought I would like to pay a small tribute to at least a few of the many funny men and women who have made me laugh over the years.

Girls growing up in the north of England in my day were all fans of Thora Hird. We felt she was one of our own, and we were proud of her. I used to go to all her films, and think she was absolutely wonderful. I always remember seeing her, when she was quite young, playing an old lady in the film, *Cure for Love*, and she delivered a particular line so well: '*Fait accompli*. I've done it. Should I have done?'

I laugh just remembering it. For an aspiring actress like me, she was a heroine. So I was thrilled when she joined the cast of *Last of the Summer Wine* and I got to work with her. Now she shares a little caravan on the moor with Jane and me when we're filming. She keeps us entertained all the time with her stories. I just love hearing about when she was a girl growing up in Morecambe in a theatrical family.

Last year a group of us from *Summer Wine* were invited to be in the audience for a special edition of Esther Rantzen's afternoon programme, *A Tribute to Dame Thora*. She went round asking us for stories about Thora, and I was getting all ready to talk about the time she had been so wonderful both in the film *A Kind of Loving* and behind the scenes, looking after Susan. But when she came to me Esther suddenly said, 'Now why don't you ever play glamorous parts on television? Looking at you now, you could quite easily get away with it.'

I was astonished. I said, 'Because I hope I can carry on playing character parts, like Thora, until I'm Thora's age. I enjoy the character parts.'

That was all I said, because she moved on to someone else then, and I didn't get the chance to pay any tribute to Thora at all, but I hope I've made amends a little now.

Then there's the incomparable Peggy Mount, another great heroine of mine. I'll never forget doing a turn at the Theatre Royal, Drury Lane, for charity, with Peggy and Doris Hare, with me dressed up as Nora Batty, and a chorus of men from all the West End shows singing, 'Standing on the corner watching all the girls go by' as we came on. At the rehearsal, when we 'girls' came on, the director said, 'No! No! No! Gentlemen! When the girls come on, you are to stop singing. Now somebody was singing when only the girls should have been singing.'

No one said anything, and then Peggy, in her deep, booming voice, said, 'Could it be me?' We all fell about.

I first saw Peggy in 1970 playing Maria in *When We*

Are Married in the West End. Gretchen Franklin played Mrs Northrop, the part I was to play at the Whitehall in 1986. Fred Emney played the photographer, great big Fred Emney. I remember going to see it with Roy Barraclough, just when we'd finished *Castle Haven* in 1970, and it cheered us both up no end. I saw Peggy in the film *Sailor Beware*. That was what really made her, that film. She was marvellous in it. I have played her part myself, the big, dominating woman, but I've also played Little Edie, the put-upon sister-in-law who is like a little terrified rabbit, crying all the time. Esme Cannon played her in the film. It was lovely for me to play that part instead of always being the strong one. Jane Freeman, my partner in crime, played the 'Peggy Mount' role. When we did the press call, the reporters all assumed that I'd be the dominant one, but I said, 'No, no. I'm Little Edie.'

I took over the role of Madam Arcati in *Blithe Spirit* from Peggy. I'd seen her in it a year before, and of course she was wonderful in it, but I didn't attempt to copy her. After my first rehearsal I said I'd go along and watch Peggy's performance again that night, before taking the role over, but the director said, 'Oh no, don't do that. Your portrayal is completely different. It might confuse you.'

Margaret Rutherford was another one who influenced me, and I saw all her films when I was young. And Cicely Courtneidge. Oh, she was just wonderful. When I was in *Two into One*, at the Shaftesbury, they had the big posters with the top of the bill's names at the top, and lower down it said, 'And Kathy Staff' with a picture of me. As I came out of my dressing room every evening there was another big poster on the wall for *Move Over Mrs Markham*. I can't tell you who the top of the bill were, but lower down it said, 'And Cicely Courtneidge' and every night I used to think, 'I've got the same billing as Cicely Courtneidge!'

Evelyn Laye was another marvellous actress, and a wonderful person to meet. I don't know why they didn't make her a dame. She was ninety-odd when she died, and I was very upset that they had never given her anything. At one time I nearly wrote to suggest it, but when you're 'in the business' yourself it's a bit difficult, because you think they'll think you're only doing it to bring yourself to their attention.

I met Evelyn Laye when she was touring in *Pygmalion* with Bill Owen, and they were coming to Birmingham. I was in *Crossroads,* and Bill said to me, 'You've got good digs in Birmingham, haven't you? Will you put a word in for me to see if I can stay there?'

It was the little Yew Tree Guest House I'd discovered, full of antiques, and you could see your face in the furniture, because it was all kept absolutely spotless, run by a lovely family. I said to Mr and Mrs Wainright that I'd given their telephone number to Bill Owen, and when I got there on the Monday they were waiting for me, absolutely thrilled to bits. They said, 'Your friend Mr Owen has booked in . . . and Evelyn Laye's coming too!'

So we all stayed at the Yew Tree Guest House together. Every evening I would wait for them to come in from the theatre, and I virtually used to sit at her feet. While she had her supper she would tell us stories about the old days, the actors, the life in the theatre – I just couldn't get enough of it.

When I was a teenager, my hero was Stewart Granger.

That voice. Then one day he came to the Manchester Opera House, to star in *Power of Darkness*. It was heavy! It was all in prison. I admired his performance, but I was worn out by the time it had finished. I suppose he was trying to prove that he could do something more than just always playing the handsome hero, but I don't think his fans appreciated it.

It's sometimes very hard to avoid being typecast, but you have to keep within some sort of bounds. I don't often get asked to play unsympathetic characters. I'd love to play the Wicked Queen, in *Snow White*, but they won't let me. They say, 'Oh no. People want to see you as a warm-hearted, loving character.' But I'd love to play a wicked person. It's just acting. Being different. Helping people to enjoy the story.

Acting has always been the thing I loved to do, the actual acting. Fame was never the spur. I was just as happy working when I was walking on as an extra as I am now. I got just the same satisfaction out of it. I think for a lot of actors fame *is* the spur. I'll never forget one day when a local girl from Dukinfield came into *Crossroads*, playing a policewoman. She only had one line. Of course, knowing her since she was a child, I was showing her round everywhere. There was a lovely kitchen where we could make tea and coffee in the greenroom, and Jane Rossington came in and said, 'Oh! Do you two know one another?'

The girl answered at once, 'Oh yes. We knew one another before we were somebody.'

That really tickled me. I thought, 'Oh yes. And who are we now, I wonder?'

Paul Henry always used to say to me that the real reason they kept me on in *Crossroads* was because I was the only one who did the washing up and kept the greenroom tidy. I did, too. I don't like to see dirty things hanging around.

I've always wanted to be the kind of actor that Alec Guinness is, because in every part he plays he not only acts differently, he even looks different. Every one. There are some big stars who, whatever part they have, play themselves. And yet he somehow loses his own personality completely, becomes a different person each time. He seems so gentle. He doesn't come across as having a big private personality. Acting all these other people somehow *is* his personality. He is exactly the sort of actor that I would like to be. I know I can't, but that is what I'd like. You become typecast and you're not given the opportunity to be different, in popular television.

Years ago, when Roy Barraclough and I were going down to London to be interviewed for *Castle Haven*, when I got to the station at Manchester and walked through on to the platform, Alec Guinness was just in front of me. I thought, 'It's an omen!' Perhaps it was. At any rate, I got the job.

Les Dawson was another hero of mine, and it was wonderful working with him. Today I think Ronnie Barker is one of the funniest, most professional men in the business. But it's quite frightening how many old friends have died, people in their prime, who you wouldn't expect, people like Les Dawson, Eric Morecambe, Tommy Cooper – brilliant stars, and not old men. I suppose they gave it their all, and literally burnt themselves out. Poor Benny Hill died in his flat, and nobody even knew he was dead. They found him days after.

I always remember when I started working with Benny Hill. Morecambe and Wise were at the peak of their fame then, and I was in make-up at Thames Television Centre when Eric Morecambe came in and sat next to me.

''Allo, Kathy.'

'Hallo.'

'Yer workin' with the tops now, y'know.'

'Oh really?'

'Oh yes. In America? Benny's Number One. His show is shown at seven thirty in the evening. They shove ours out at eleven fifteen. Nobody watches us.'

He was quite right. I've heard only recently that they want to do a three-hour *Benny Hill Spectacular*, a put-together of all the old shows, on American television. I remember when I was first asked to be on, Henry McGee, who was always with Benny as his straight man, saying to me, 'Never mind the fee, dear, if it's small. Wait until you see the repeats you get.' I wondered whatever he meant, but he was right. In America they repeat it and repeat it. I still get money nearly every month for the work I did with Benny Hill.

Another funny man is Mike Craig. He was writer and producer of *The Grumbleweeds* radio show and had me as a guest four times. In one sketch I was Cinderella, but instead of a glass slipper I wore a glass corset, which shattered when I put it on. He invited me as a guest on a comedy cruise on the *Canberra* three years ago with *The Grumbleweeds*. We had a fantastic time. He was a very funny compère and did an act about all the old variety comedians. He has now started a 'lunch and laughter' club, where we can listen to some of our top comedians like Tom O'Connor, Ken Dodd, Norman Collier, etc. It is great.

28

Not the *Last*
of the Summer Wine

In this book I've sometimes given the programme
its proper title, *Last of the Summer Wine*, but quite
often I've called it what most people do, just *Summer
Wine*. Unfortunately, because people are so used to
referring to it as *Summer Wine*, the newspapers have
been reporting for *years* that each series is the last one,
when they see it written as *Last of the Summer Wine*.
In fact, even as I write, we start filming next week for
next year, the beginning of the next quarter-century.

We can't believe it. We can't believe how it's gone
on and on.

The years have just flown. When we started we were
all younger than the characters we played. Now some of
us have caught up, and some are much older than their
parts. Nora was in her sixties when I was only in my
forties, but I've caught her up now. Bill is eighty-three
this year, so he's overtaken Compo. Thora's eighty-six.
And yet we're all meant to be contemporaries; we
all went to school together. And Jane Freeman, that
lovely round girlish face, with her hair scraped down
trying to look older at the beginning, now even she's
grown into it.

It's a good job that I wasn't Nora's age when we
started. Wally Batty's motor-bike and sidecar didn't

have a door, so I had to clamber over the bike to get in. I doubt I could do that now. After Joe died I thought I should leave. I think the women each need to have 'a little man' to play opposite, and it has been much less enjoyable without Wally, and I've had much less to do. But they persuaded me to stay. So then I hoped that Roy Clarke would write in another little man, someone like Howard, as my lodger, and have him working by day at the cafe with Jane. She has lost her husband Sid, and her nephew, Crusher, so she's in the same position as me – no little man to control. I still think it's a pity we didn't do that. Howard would have been bullied at both ends of his day. Nora and Ivy could really have made his whole life a total misery, more even than Pearl manages, and the three men would have been trying constantly to help him escape.

There have only ever been four directors, which has helped *Summer Wine* to endure, and the setting and the scenery make it attractive to look at. Above all, it's the writing that's so good. Roy Clarke has created a world with time suspended in one long perpetual summer, somewhere in the late sixties or early seventies, with a group of sixty-something men and women, all of the generation who would have served in the Second World War.

Roy says that when the BBC first asked him to write a comedy about three retired men, he couldn't think of anything funny at all. He said, 'I kept thinking I couldn't do it. Nothing seemed funny. Suddenly, it came to me – it could be like second childhood. And I thought, "That's it! There are three old men, free from all responsibilities, trying to keep on doing the things they used to do."'

Later, he said one of the nicest things to me, 'It's never ceased to amaze me, the way you've made Nora Batty into a main character. I only put her in originally to lead to Compo, never thinking she would ever make anything.'

In spite of the 'timelessness', some things have changed over the years. Compo was much more dirty and repulsive in the early days . . . you could nearly smell him. He's more refined now, partly because of Bill's lovely snowy white hair. When it was dark it looked more disgusting and dirty. Now it's gone white, it's such a pure white. For a long time they didn't allow him to wash it, but now he does, and it looks so clean under that little woolly cap. And Bill Owen gives him such charm underneath the repulsiveness, which is why Nora Batty can never quite say, 'Go away' and really mean it. She still hankers a little bit, and wants to mother him. If Compo ignored Nora, and stopped pestering her, she really would be upset. The women in *Summer Wine* all need their men.

The three men all have stand-in 'doubles' these days, a stuntman for anything that's really dangerous, and a 'double' for wide shots of things that are very strenuous. But some scenes just can't be faked by a double. In the latest series, I had a scene with Compo, standing on his head. When I read the script I thought, 'I wonder how they're going to do this.'

My lines were, 'What are you doin' down there?' and, 'Oh! Well, it's better than the right way up, I suppose.' They did have his 'double' upside down when I was saying my lines, but Bill had to be really standing on his head to deliver his own lines. Someone was holding him, of course, but even so. He's eighty-three, you know. You have to hand it to him.

It's the same when he's been up on the roof. They can use a 'double' for a long shot of him walking along, but for a close-up of him saying the lines with his face near the chimney, he has to get up there himself. And whenever we're doing a scene where I'm throwing water at him, he insists on doing that himself. He loves it. I've said to him, 'Bill, why ever don't you let your stand-in do it?' but he always says, 'Oh no. It's funnier if they see me close up being wet through.' Of course, he's right, it is.

Cleggy has always been the philosopher of the three men. In the very first episode he had a line, 'Who's going to do the thinking if we are not?' Roy says that Cleggy is really him. And Roy Clarke's wife, Enid, always used to say to me, '*I'm* Nora Batty, you know. I'm the real Nora Batty. It's me.'

I think she did keep him in order. I think there was something in it.

After we'd been going for the first twenty-one years, the BBC held a dinner to celebrate the longest running comedy series ever, and they gave a certificate to the four of us who have been in it from the beginning: Jane Freeman, Bill Owen, Peter Sallis and myself, and of course they gave Roy one. There was a dinner, and Roy's wife Enid was there. I've always loved Enid. They always used to come along when we were filming, and give us a party at the end of each series. She was a very attractive and vivacious blonde, but she still always reckoned he'd written Nora based on her.

At this party for the twenty-first, Enid was sitting next to me, wearing a shawl, and I don't know why, but I started telling her about Katherine having had cancer. She was so sympathetic and kind, and she said, 'You look after that girl.'

I said, 'I will. It was terrible, because I was in Scotland, and I wanted to come right down . . .' and she said, 'Yes, I can understand that.'

I don't know why, because I'd never told any of the others about Katherine, but when I was talking to Enid, it all came out. But then she said, 'I can't move my arm. That's why I've got it under this shawl. So nobody can see. I think I must have trapped a nerve or something.'

A few weeks later, Alan Bell rang me and said, 'Roy doesn't want anybody else to know, but I know how friendly you are with Roy and Enid, and she's in hospital. I thought you should know.' It was a brain tumour.

John and I went over immediately to see her in hospital in Sheffield, where she'd just had an operation. They'd shaved off all her lovely blonde hair, and she was sitting up in bed with her shaved head. I've never been hugged so long in all my life. She sobbed and hung on to me and said, 'Oh, it's lovely to see you. Fancy you coming all this way.'

She told me that they'd operated on the tumour on the brain, but they said there was another one on her lungs, but they'd leave that one for a bit. She did make a sort of recovery and they sent her home. I used to go and see her and ring her up, so I knew how things were progressing. One day she said to me, 'Kathy, my arm and my leg have gone again. And that can't be in my lungs, can it?' She died shortly after.

The last thing Enid said to me when she was leaving the twenty-first anniversary party, was, 'Now you look after that girl of yours, I'm telling you.' She was a lovely, lovely lady.

Our oldest and most loyal viewer must be a friend of ours, Louie Aspland, who lives at Lytham St Annes, with her niece, Ethel Fieldhouse. Louie used to live in Dukinfield, on Astley Street, just further down from us, and she was the Sunday-school teacher at St Mark's. She taught my mother, she taught Con and me, and she was still there, playing the piano, when Katherine and Susan went to Sunday school. The first bike that Con and I ever had was Louie's old bike, that my mother bought from her second-hand.

Louie was one hundred and nine years old in March. Ethel, who looks after her, is eighty-five. Louie has always loved *Summer Wine*. Her eyesight isn't very good any more, so she gets a cushion on the floor so that she can sit next to the screen and see it. So I'm sure she must be our oldest, most faithful fan.

And now we've all just celebrated twenty-five years. A quarter of a century of *Summer Wine*. Of one thing I'm quite certain, we won't be going on for another twenty-five years. None of us can go on for ever, so it's bound to come to an end eventually. It's been a wonderful thing to have been in from the beginning, knowing that it has given so much pleasure. Mine was the very first line in it. I hope I'll be there to deliver the very last line one day.

Afterword

I'm asked to give many more after-lunch and after-dinner speeches than I can manage to accept. I enjoy myself when I get there, but I always wonder if they are expecting me to be a comedian. I'm not. I just talk, going through my career picking out various things, usually the more amusing things. I don't dwell on the sad things. And they always seem to enjoy it. I hope they do.

I find praise a bit embarrassing. I never think of myself as 'famous'. I just feel the same as I've always felt. I haven't been round the world or had tea with the Queen or won the OBE. I couldn't believe it when I got the letter from the publisher. I said to John, 'Look at this! They want me to write a book – about me!'

I always feel I'm so normal, so ordinary, quite a boring person really, so what interest is my life to anyone else? There have been no dramas. No great tragedies. Just living through the things we all have to go through day by day.

I didn't know if Hodder and Stoughton had done the right thing, asking me to write my life story, but now I'm glad they did, because I've enjoyed doing it very much. Liz Barr, my co-writer, has become a good new friend. It's brought back memories of old friends, who are always there, in my heart, but it's nice to talk about them and tell others about the people and events that have been important to me and my family.

I have seen a lot of changes in the world of acting. When I started, every town had its own repertory theatre, so all aspiring young actors were doing weekly rep. You could get work, perhaps as an assistant stage-manager, and work your way up, and learn your trade that way. Today they really have to go to theatre school, and when they've finished there's still no guarantee of work. They've spent two or three years training hard, and then they're just right at the bottom of the pile, without even the chance of working for peanuts, like I did.

There are still some repertory theatres, but far fewer, and they aren't the same as they were when I was young. Oldham Rep had ten or twelve actors, who were in all the plays. Now you don't see your favourite actor this week playing one thing, and next week playing something completely different. You get touring plays brought in, with different people coming from all over the place.

On the other hand, there are a lot of new openings, not in the theatres, but in television and radio. That didn't really exist when I was starting. There was no television before the war, and very little for the first few years after the war.

I started as a professional actress in 1949, when there was still no television work to speak of. I remember that when the Queen was married we listened to it on the radio. By the time she was crowned in 1953 there was television, and everyone went to friends to watch it. Anybody with a television set suddenly had a lot of friends. Auntie Doris and Uncle Clem, the butcher, had a little set. It must only have been a nine-inch screen, and all the Higginbottom brothers went to watch it, my Mum and Dad went, and they must all have been so squashed up, sitting round this tiny screen.

Today television is the main employer for actors, and I just hope that all these new television channels will make a lot of work, and not just show endless repeats, because we have so many talented young people coming up in the business who don't get given enough opportunities. Television, once they've established somebody, tends to use them over and over again. Television people don't like to take the risk with unknowns.

Of course, I did enter television on the bottom rung myself, going in as an extra, even though I had had a lot of stage experience. Perhaps if young people are prepared to start like that, they might stand a chance. Sometimes extra work is more difficult than a small part, because you are asked to react to something, and you've no lines, only your face and body to react with, which can be much harder than saying a line. And it can pay off. If you gradually become known to the producers' assistants and assistant directors as a reliable and enthusiastic actor, and if you are always prepared to be there on time and to work hard, even for your non-speaking part, it may well lead to better things. It certainly did for me.

John has been happy, I think. His father was right when he said there would be more opportunities for him in Manchester. He thoroughly enjoyed his career, and worked to the top of the tree. He wouldn't have wanted to be a headmaster, because they don't do any teaching, but he was head of the mathematics department at Audenshaw Grammar School. He had a very successful and happy career teaching at the sort of school he was used to, with all boys.

He says he doesn't miss it now. He finds plenty to do, dealing with all the business side of my work. There's an amazing amount of paperwork that needs doing.

I don't know what a modern accountant with all their whizz-bang computers would say about John's Audenshaw Grammar School exercise books, all done by hand, but he could tell you everything I've ever done, what it was, how much I got paid, when it was repeated. He's got all the information at his fingertips, and that has been an enormous help to me in getting things right for this book.

John calls himself my roadie now. Especially now he's retired, he usually drives me everywhere. I'm a punctual and well-organised person. I can't bear to be late, and that is one thing that sets me into a panic. If we get stuck in a traffic jam, that is the only time when I can almost lose my self-control. I'll yell at him, 'Can't we find any other way? Let's go some other way!'

And he'll say, 'Now calm down.'

And he gets me there. He's always got me there.

I really don't know what I would like my epitaph to be. 'She was a good Christian mum', perhaps. That's been the most important role of my life. It's the role that you don't shake off. It's the role you play twenty-four hours a day. It's not like Nora Batty. You can take the rollers out and the apron and wrinkled stockings off, and she's just a heap on the floor. Being a Mum has been the important thing. I hope I've done it right.